Robert J. (Robert James) Turnbull

A Visit to the Philadelphia Prison

Being an Accurate and Particular Account of the Wise and...

Robert J. (Robert James) Turnbull

A Visit to the Philadelphia Prison
Being an Accurate and Particular Account of the Wise and...

ISBN/EAN: 9783744797245

Printed in Europe, USA, Canada, Australia, Japan

Cover: Foto ©Suzi / pixelio.de

More available books at **www.hansebooks.com**

V I S I T

TO THE

PHILADELPHIA PRISON;

Being an accurate and particular Account

Of the Wife and Humane Adminiftration

Adopted in every Part of that Building ;

CONTAINING ALSO

AN ACCOUNT OF THE GRADUAL REFORMATION

AND PRESENT

IMPROVED STATE,

OF THE

PENAL LAWS OF PENNSYLVANIA:

WITH

OBSERVATIONS

ON THE

IMPOLICY AND INJUSTICE

OF

CAPITAL PUNISHMENTS.

In a LETTER to a FRIEND.

By ROBERT J. TURNBULL,

OF SOUTH CAROLINA.

" Vitiorum femina—otium—labore exhauriendum."

D U B L I N :

Printed by Robert Napper,

FOR JOHN GOUGH, NO. 20, MEATH-STREET.

M.DCC.XCVIII.

PREFACE.

THE following sheets originally made their appearance in the CHARLESTOWN Daily Gazette, some time in the month of February last; and are now republished with the addition of the notes, tables, and such alterations in various parts of the text, as have been suggested to the author on a further review of the subject.

The propriety of their coming forward in the style in which they now appear, will be readily conceived by the reader, on being acquainted that they were never designed for publication, even in the first instance. Communicated to a distant friend, merely as the result of a few leisure observations on an institution, for some time past the admiration of all strangers, the author had no desire (nor indeed expectation) that they should be perused, excepting by a few particular friends. The gentleman, however, to whom they were written, perhaps from a partiality to the author, considered them so far useful and entertaining as to have sent them to the Editors of the Gazette. The circumstance likewise of Governor Vanderhorst's having not long before offered his ideas on the same subject, to the legislature of South Carolina, probably furnished him with an additional reason, why they should not be withheld from his fellow citizens.

With

With refpect to the anecdotal facts contained in the publication, relative to the interior management of the prifon, they have all fallen under the immediate obfervation of the writer ; while the tables, and other information on the fame head, have been extracted and collected either from the dockets or other records and documents of the prifon, or from perfonal converfations with the infpectors. The whole, however, may be relied on as minutely accurate and authentic, as the manufcript was feveral weeks for perufal in the hands of two infpectors, to whofe attention and care in pointing out the errors, the author begs leave to offer once more his fincere acknowledgments.

On the fecond fubject embraced in the letter, that is, the *inefficacy of a fanguinary code*, it is fufficient to obferve, that as mankind in general have long been the dupes and victims, to all the mifchiefs of fuperftition and falfe fyftems of religion, fo have they been more or lefs affected, from a blindly adopted policy in matters of jurifprudence. How far the following reafoning in the theory, and many evidences from practice, may eftablifh this pofition, the reader muft determine ; with a recollection at the fame time, that as the fame of a writer has been the moft diftant object of the author, all imperfections in ftyle muft be candidly overlooked—His aim has uniformly been to be as extenfively ufeful to thofe around him, as fituation and circumftances would admit ; and fhould he, in this firft emanation of a youthful pen, acquire but a partial fuccefs, the reflection of having contributed in fome fmall degree to the benefit of the community, of which he is a member, will prove a grateful reward.

Philadelphia, 4th Auguft, 1796.

A

V I S I T

TO THE

PHILADELPHIA PRISON, &c.

AMONG the various communications made by
your governor to the legiflature, in the early
part of their late feffion, I was not a little pleafed to
obferve, that an alteration of the penal code of the
ftate, by mitigating the prefent punifhments, was an
object which he particularly preffed as commanding
their attention. That every degree of humanity
fhould be mingled in the organization of laws for the
prevention of crimes, by annexing as mild penalties
as poffible to the tranfgreffion of them, is a truth no
lefs confiftent with the refined principles of reafon
and morality, than it accords with the true interefts
and wifhes of that community whom the legiflature
is defigned to reprefent. And to perceive the re-
commendation of the executive magiftrate of a government, influenced by a fentiment *, which, while

---

* Vide that part of Governor Vanderhorft's meffage to the
South Carolina legiflature, wherein he recommends a fort and
other public works to be completed by the labour of criminals
on the Ifland of Marfh, oppofite the city of Charleftown, called
Shute's Folly.

it

it reflects honour on him as a philanthropist, will, if adopted, contribute so materially to the public happiness, must afford the most pleasing consolation to every feeling mind.

You are already, my dear friend, too well acquainted with my thoughts on the subject, to make it now necessary to assure you, of my personal satisfaction at this official proposal of a system, which has existed till lately in theory only, and whose beauties should have so long and so generally escaped the attention of the humane. While so many arts have been invented, and the principles of every science discovered by the ingenuity of men; while, combined with their intellectual faculties, they find stamped on them the grand moral attribute of fellow-feeling; that so few should have exerted themselves, to put in practice some plan or other for reducing to a reasonable standard, those sanguinary codes of laws so prevalent throughout the globe, appears to me a circumstance not altogether accounted for. Surely nothing but a blind prejudice to customs, engendered in the depression of human happiness by ignorance, and the inexorable scourge of tyranny, could have given countenance to a policy like this. But in an age like the present, and in a country like our own, when burst from the chains which have long and cruelly bound it, the mind of man is once more accessible to the mild influence of reason and humanity, how strange that a rigour of the kind should exist. Thanks however to the virtue of Americans, that efforts towards the total abolition of it have not been wanting in this western hemisphere. Pennsylvania has pointed out the necessity of the measure; directed by the unerring guidance of hitherto unexampled wisdom, she has furnished to the world an instance of good sense and virtue, which must redound to her honour, for ages yet in the womb of
time,

time, and when her fister ftates fhall follow her foot-fteps, then and not till then, will the rifing empire of America have completed its happinefs on the bafis of genuine liberty.

Premifing thus much, and in further compliance with my promife of writing, I am neceffarily induced to give you an account of the Philadelphia Prifon. Notwithftanding a refidence in this place for fome months, I had never the curiofity till the laft week, to vifit this WONDER of the world. The expreffion is comprehenfive but no lefs juft; for, of all the Bridewells or Penitentiary Houfes I ever read or heard of, I have met with none founded on fimilar princi-ples, or which could in any manner boaft of an ad-miniftration fo extenfively ufeful and humane.

Externally this prifon prefents itfelf as a very ftrong and fecure building, conftructed of ftone, with a ground floor and two ftories; and rather refembling an incomplete hollow parallelogram than any other form, with a north front on Walnut, and a fouth one on Prune-ftreet. The principal front on Walnut-ftreet meafures one hundred and ninety feet in length, and forty feet in depth. The eaft and weft fides or wings of the fame depth, refpectively, extend at right angles with the main front, ninety-five feet in a fouthern direction, and then join ftone walls of twenty feet in height, running to the fouth-eaft and fouth-weft corners. The weft wing is on South Sixth-ftreet. Thefe three fides are appropriated for the confinement of criminals, vagrants, &c. and whofe outward appearance does not much refemble a prifon, but neat, handfome, and no inconfiderable ornament to the city.

Nearly contiguous to the eaft wing, is a brick edifice of two ftories, raifed upon arches, of about forty feet in length, and twenty-five in breadth, fet apart for the purpofe of folitary confinement. The fouth

fouth front on Prune-ftreet is partly the wall, and
partly the debtor's apartment, a ftone building originally intended for a work-houfe, about forty-five feet
in length, and fifty-five in depth. The whole of the
buildings ftand on a lot of two hundred feet by four
hundred; one hundred feet of the fouth part of
which, is divided off for the ufe of the debtors by a
wall running eaft and weft.

Having been previoufly prepared with a permit,
procured by a friend from one of the Committee of
Infpectors, to vifit the prifon, we delivered it at the
door, when orders were immediately given to a turnkey, to conduct us through the different parts of it.
We were firft fhewn through the grand entry, fecured
by an iron grated door about midway, and from
thence (acrofs a court or paffage running from one
end of the front to the other) directly into the yard
of the prifon. Conceive, my friend, the pleafant fenfations which by turns took poffeffion of our minds at
the time, when I declare, that inftead of having our
eyes palled, as we might naturally expect, by the
gloomy appearance of the walls of a jail-yard, we
found ourfelves amidft a fmall induftrious community.
At the fouth-weft corner of the yard ftood a wooden
building, in which is eftablifhed a manufactory of
nails on an extenfive plan. Here are manufactured
cut nails of all defcriptions, and particularly brads of
an excellent quality; the whole by a method eafy
and expeditious. We were informed by the fuperin-
tendant of this manufactory, that about five hundred
weight of nails were daily produced by the labour of
the criminals.

Next to the manufactory is a blackfmith's fhop,
while in other parts of the yard are erected fmall
fheds, where the occupations of fawing marble,
cutting ftone, &c. were purfued in their refpective
branches. In fhort there was fuch a fpirit of induftry
visible

vifible on every fide, and fuch contentment pervaded the countenances of all, that it was with difficulty I divefted myfelf of the idea, that thefe men *furely were not* convicts, but accuftomed to labour from their infancy.

Previous to proceeding further with an account of the prifon and its government, it will here be necef-fary to digrefs and remind you, that the criminal laws of Pennfylvania, are eftablifhed on fo firm a foundation of lenity, as to abrogate the punifhment of death for every crime except cool and deliberate murder. On the firft emigration to, and fettlement of the country by William Penn, the charter from king Charles the Second, ftrictly enjoined the eftablifhment of the ftatute and common law of the mother-country. This was ill relifhed by fuch a friend of the human race as Penn, and the principles of whofe fect de-manded with firmnefs, the compilation of a more mild and rational code of criminal laws. In obedience therefore to thofe injunctions, and others dictated by a pure and enlightened mind, he engaged in the tafk, and produced a fyftem, which confined the lofs of life, as a punifhment for deliberate murder only. This departure however, as might be expected, met with little or no encouragement in England ; on the new code being tranfmitted to Queen Anne for royal approbation (as was ufually done with all laws, and indeed required by the charter) it met with her de-cided difpleafure, and was confequently annulled. It was notwithftanding fome fhort time after again enacted, and continued in force for upwards of thirty years, when a very long and warm difpute on the fame fubject, having arifen between the governor of the colony and the throne, the latter fucceeded, and infifted upon and eftablifhed the laws prefcribed in the charter, in their fulleft extent.

In this fituation did affairs remain, until the bands of connection between Great Britain and America

were

were diffolved by the declaration of independence. Then in the full poffeffion of a liberty, the profpect of which had induced the original inhabitants of Pennfylvania to fly from Europe, the revival of the former penal code, which had remained in fo long and obfcure an oblivion, was immediately deemed an object of the firft importance. As fuch, it engaged the attention not only of the Quakers, but of a confiderable proportion of other claffes of citizens. Several circumftances combined, to make the propofed alteration expedient, and among others, the fmall and valuable gift of the immortal Beccaria to the world, had its due influence and weight; for on the framing of the (then) new conftitution of the ftate, in 1776, the legiflature were directed *to proceed as foon as might be, to the reformation of the penal laws, and to invent punifhments lefs fanguinary, and better proportioned to the various degrees of criminality.* The ravages of a ruinous and unnatural conflict, with the fubfequent diftrefs occafioned by it, in a great degree poftponed the carrying into effect thefe humane intentions, till the year 1786, when the foundation of this longdefired reform was at length laid by an act of the legiflature. By this act a mitigation was fo far accomplifhed, as to referve the punifhment of death for four crimes, namely, murder, rape, arfon, and treafon; while all other offences were directed to be punifhed with whipping, imprifonment, and hard labour. Unfortunately however, for the friends of humanity, the new fyftem of mildnefs was far from having the juftice of a fair experiment, and was found by no means to embrace the views of its fupporters. The number of convicts had in fome degree diminifhed, but in fo *very* trifling a proportion, as not to render it an object worthy of legiflative attention, to continue leffening the then exifting feverity. A grand and important defect, though not generally obferved, appeared too plain to fome of the promoters of the

plan,

plan, to infpire them with fanguine expectations of its fuccefs. It was the inefficacy of the punifhments of public labour, mutilation and whipping, inafmuch as they deftroyed an important end of punifhment, that of the criminal's reformation. Too fatally was this experienced! The convicts who were fentenced to the wheel-barrow, and chained and difperfed along the ftreets and roads, exhibited, from the difficulty of fuperintending them, the moft fhameful fcenes of drunkennefs, indelicacy, and other exceffes in vice. The inconveniences and mifchievous effects of the punifhment of public labour, at length became fo intolerable, that it was regarded, and with much juftice, as a common nuifance. In confequence of which, complaints againft the alteration of the ancient penal code became daily more univerfal, and fo much fo at one time, as to threaten almoft immediate deftruction to all the fchemes of the humane.

The Quakers had been the original advocates for the profcription of feverity. The fame motives which had uniformly diftinguifhed the character of thefe people in their fupport of all charitable inftitutions, induced them ftill to keep the lead in a purfuit, equally noble and praife-worthy. Their fpirit of perfeverance then, when they had in contemplation the advancement of good order and humanity, was not to fubfide, even at this provoking trial of difcouragement. The rapid growth and magnitude of the evil, ferved rather as a new incentive to awaken them more, and to convince them, that without indefatigable pains their important ends could never be accomplifhed. Neceffity, which generally and bountifully gives a new tone and vigour to the genius, was not in this inftance dilatory in the production of a remedy. Aided by other refpectable and influential characters of the community, the Quakers formed themfelves into a fociety *for alleviating the miferies of public prifons*, the object of which was, to inquire

into

into the abuses of prisons and public places of confinement, and to report them to the legislature, with a petition for redress; and also to examine the influence of confinement or imprisonment, on the morals of the persons who were the subjects of them.

The exertions of the society, after considerable opposition, procured from the legislature an amendment to the penal code, by an act of the 5th of April, 1790, which abolished the former punishments, and established in lieu of them, *private* labour, fine and imprisonment. This law, it may be said, was *forced* from the legislature; for nothing but their confidence in the individuals who composed this association, could have persuaded them to risk a further experiment. Anticipating few or no good consequences from the substitution of a mild discipline, instead of death, severity and irons, they thought it prudent, and took care to limit the existence of the law, for the space of five years. The act, after laying down several general regulations for the government of prisons, entrusts in the hands of a board of inspectors, " the power of making, at their quarterly or other meetings, such further orders and regulations, for the purpose of carrying the act into execution, as should be approved by the mayor and recorder of the city." By a supplement to the act, passed in Sept. 1791, the same power is transferred from the mayor and recorder, to the mayor, two aldermen, and two of the judges of the supreme court, or two of the judges of the court of common pleas of Philadelphia county.

I hinted, that a considerable opposition had disputed the establishment of this mitigated mode of treatment. It existed for a length of time; and the most powerful proceeded, not so much from ignorance, prejudice, or want of benevolence (for its opposers were respectable and humane), as from the trifling prospect and hope, which a mistaken and too despicable opinion of persons

sons

fons guilty of offences had led many to have and en-
tertain of its fortunate iffue.

Among the fervices of feveral perfons, who early
formed an attachment to the principles of the fociety,
thofe of the late attorney-general of the United States,
the worthy and much refpected William Bradford,
deceafed, are fufficiently well known to merit the
recollection and gratitude of his countrymen. Being
at that time judge of the commonwealth of Pennfylvania, he had occafion to differ on this point, with
his brethren on the bench, who denied their confent
from none but the pureft and moft patriotic motives,
fuch as their tried knowledge of crimes and criminals
had prompted them confcientioufly to refpect. On
the firft appearance of the favourable fymptoms which
the triumph of their adverfaries had effected in the
government and conduct of the prifoners, they coin-
cided, and afterwards contributed much to its maintenance.

In juftice to other refpectable perfons, not of the
Quaker perfuafion, it may here be mentioned, that
notwithftanding that fect were, in general, the principal fupporters of every improvement on the new
fyftem, ftill the caufe was always warmly efpoufed by
other citizens. Nor can it be contradicted, that
among the prefent number of them there are feveral
whofe humane labours have not been exceeded. To
pafs over the conduct of the enlightened Doctor
Benjamin Rufh, might properly be deemed an act of
omiffion. Although the preffing duties of his profeffion called for his humane affiftance in other quar-
ters, he was no lefs eager to appropriate occafionally,
a few leifure hours, on the fubject of a fcheme fo
pregnant with the future happinefs of millions, and
which fimply required public fpirit and perfeverance
to deliver to *mankind*. With this view he came
forward at a very critical juncture, and publifhed a
fmall pamphlet, called " An Inquiry into the Effects
" of

" of public Punifhments upon Criminals and Society;" in which, after difplaying with a philofophic calmnefs, the greateft acquaintance with the fprings of the human heart, he fully demonftrates their inutility and mifchievous tendency. A few years growth of the fyftem which abolifhed them, has already eftablifhed the truth of his principles.

Upon the whole, the promoters of this laft grand work of philanthropy met with fo much fuccefs in the experiment, and its operations produced fo vifible a change in the criminal dockets throughout the ftate, that the legiflature, fo far from fuffering their intended temporary law to expire without renewal, extended their lenity ftill further, and by the memorable act of the 22d of April, 1794, abolifhed the punifhment of death for every crime, excepting murder of the firft degree. Any kind of murder perpetrated by means of poifon, by laying in wait, or by any other kind of wilful, deliberate, and premeditated killing, committed in the perpetration, or attempt to perpetrate, any arfon, rape, robbery, or burglary, is declared to be murder of the firft degree. Perfons guilty of other offences are therefore now divided into claffes. Of the firft clafs are all perfons guilty of offences, which, previous to the paffing of the law, were punifhable with death ; and alfo thofe guilty of other heinous offences mentioned in the act. Thefe undergo a punifhment compounded of hard labour and folitary confinement, for a certain term of years. Thofe of the fecond clafs, are convicts condemned for offences lefs criminal, who are merely fubjected to hard labour. As to the meafure for each particular crime or mifdemeanor, it is principally difcretionary with the judges of the court, before whom they are tried, under the reftrictions laid down in the firft of the fubjoined tables.

With thefe prefaratory obfervations on the nature, progrefs, and gradual improvement, of the criminal

laws

laws of Pennfylvania, I fhall be more in order to
proceed with my defcription of the prifon. From
viewing the yard, our curiofity naturally led us to
examine the interior apartments of the building. We
firft went through the ground-floor, or front half-
ftory, chiefly appropriated for kitchens, which were
exceedingly clean. Some men were bufily employed
in carrying plaifter of Paris in lumps along this paffage, to an apartment in the eaft end of the ftory,
where it is ground by others, in a mill fixed for the
purpofe. There were feveral other rooms, but nothing material engaged our notice.

We next afcended the firft whole ftory, with which
there is no communication with the under, except by
a flight of fteps outfide in the yard. At the back part
of this, as well as the other floors, there are long
courts or paffages, extending from one end of the
front to the other, about the width of twelve feet.
Along the paffage here, are ranged eight apartments,
three of which being occupied as the apartments of
the jailer, and one made ufe of as the infpector's room,
have no entrance to them withinfide of the iron-
grated door. The reft open into the paffage, and
are work-fhops, with inftruments and tools for carpenters, joiners, turners, fhoemakers, weavers, and
taylors. Thefe different trades we faw carried on
with all the induftry imaginable. There were alfo
perfons in the court, employed in chipping logwood.
The work-fhops are of the dimenfions of twenty feet
by nineteen feet; neat, healthy, and airy; perfectly
fecure from fire and an efcape, by being arched over
with ftone, and having double iron gratings to the
windows. No communication with them can be
effected by perfons in the ftreet.

The upper ftory contains the fame number of rooms,
ranged in like manner as the lower apartments; the
firft of which, at the weft end, is fet apart as an
infirmary, for the reception of fick prifoners, and the
reft

reſt bed rooms. In each of the rooms are about one dozen beds with mattreſſes, ſheets, and rugs; every priſoner being allowed a ſingle bed. All theſe front ſtories are appropriated for none but male convicts.

The firſt ſtory of the eaſt wing contains five apartments, conſtructed in the ſame manner, in which are confined perſons accuſed and committed for trial, who are not made to labour. In the ſecond, or upper ſtory, are the vagrants, and runaway ſervants. Theſe perſons are employed in beating hemp, picking moſs, hair, wool, or oakum. There is a court-yard to this wing, meaſuring ninety by thirty-two feet.

We next viſited the apartments of the women, in the weſt wing of the priſon, on Sixth-ſtreet. The ground floor of this wing was formerly divided off into dungeons; but now are ſeldom, or never entered, unleſs to ſtow away wood, or any bulky material.— In the firſt ſtory are four rooms, ranged in the ſame manner as thoſe of the eaſt wing, appropriated for the uſe of the female convicts; beſides another, uſed as a ſtore-room for the articles manufactured in the houſe. The women perform their labour in the paſſage; they were engaged, ſome in ſpinning cotton and mop yarn, carding wool, picking cotton, ſewing, and preparing flax and hemp; others in waſhing and mending. They have a court-yard, of the ſame dimenſions of the one belonging to the untried criminals, and male vagrants. In the upper ſtory of this wing are confined female vagrants, and women of bad character, who are alſo kept at profitable employments.

You muſt admire, my friend, the excellency of theſe arrangements. You perceive, in the firſt place, there is no intercourſe whatever between the males and females; they cannot even ſee each other. None again between convicted and untried criminals; nor between either of them and the vagrants. This muſt at all times be a deſirable object. Perſons who have

not

not been convicted of the charges they stand im-
prisoned for, ought not, in justice, to have a connection with, and be placed among, such prisoners as
have been condemned. The difference of their
situation demands a separation. On the other hand,
as the intention of the new system of laws is not only
to punish offenders, but to restore them reformed to
society, it is more absolutely necessary, that the
convicts should be kept apart from the vagrants.

It is well known, that in no one place are offered
more injurious and vicious examples, than in a prison,
where condemned, untried, and all other classes of
prisoners, are intermingled, without regard either to
age, sex, or condition. Those in many parts of
Europe, and several in America, have long stood
melancholy evidences of this fact. Thousands are
committed annually for a trifling fault, or misdemea-
nor—many from misfortune, or accident—and we
may venture to assert, that scarcely one has been
dismissed, with the same stock of morality he carried
in with him. Accustomed to idleness, debauchery,
and practice of frauds upon their keepers, upon
visiters, and upon each other, the young and unex-
perienced criminal is early taught to imitate the
dexterity of his elders—the timorous soon acquires
the audacity of his more hardened companions—the
modest become spectators of, and inured to the indelicacy and indecency of others—and thus, amidst such
frequent opportunities for vice, are planned, not a
trifling proportion of the murders, robberies, and
other kinds of villany, perpetrated after their escape
or discharge.

In Philadelphia, the *separation* of the different
classes of prisoners was early deemed an object of
the highest importance, by all who were in any wise
interested in the then contemplated reform of the
prison government, and as such steadily adhered to.
The inhabitants of the prison were extremely averse

to

to the meafure, and were always more emboldened in their confidence of its failing, from the countenance of their jailer and keepers, who naturally preferred the old fyftem, as it would furnifh them with a greater harveft of perquifites and exactions. Finding at length that the perfeverance of " the fociety for " alleviating the miferies of prifons," bid fair to an extinction of all hopes of their continuing in the fame fcene of confufion, with one confent they refolved on a breach of prifon. The attempt was accordingly made on the evening of the day the new order of things had taken place. Fortunately few of them efcaped. The jailer was immediately difcharged, and fince that period almoft every project for the fame purpofe has failed, either from the want of unanimity of the moft evil difpofed, the fears of thofe lefs fo, or the decided difapprobation of the greateft propor-tion of the prifoners, to any thing of the kind.

Nothing appears more grievous to a perfon, long initiated into habits of indolence and licentioufnefs, than the idea of being compelled to alter them. This I hold as an undoubted pofition; and therefore the conftant and hard labour, to which a criminal is fentenced in Pennfylvania, muft be productive (and it has been) of the moft beneficial effects. Although humane, it is a punifhment, fufficiently dreadful and fevere to excite terror into the minds of the depraved; and, befides affording an example of true juftice, it is of all others the beft adapted for the amendment of the convict himfelf. Another thing; as the defign of penalties is not only to prevent the commiffion of crimes, and reform offenders, but likewife to make reparation for the injury done to fociety, or one of its members; the laft of thefe objects, cannot be better obtained, than by the perfonal induftry of the criminal, while under condemnation. Of this the legiflature were no doubt fully perfuaded, when they
fell

fell upon the prefent improvement, in matters of jurifprudence.

The proceeds of the labour and fervices of the delinquent are not, in every inftance, applied to the ufe of the injured public, or individual. For if after making the reparation required by his fentence ; that is, if at the expiration of his confinement, and after paying the expenfes of his commitment, profecution, and trial ; the value of articles ftolen, or damage done to the profecutor ; the fine to the commonwealth ; hire of the tools he makes ufe of ; and, laftly, the expenfes of his board, clothing, wafhing, and lodging, any balance, or overplus, is found to remain, or be due to him, it is either paid to him in cafh or clothing. The fine to the commonwealth is generally remitted.

- That part of the fentence, including the cofts and expenfes of profecution, and alfo the expenfes of feeding and clothing a convict, are advanced by the county in which he takes his trial, and are afterwards repaid by the induftry of the criminal. When the prifoners fent to the prifon, from other counties, have incurred a charge for their maintenance, more than the profits of their labour will defray, they are reported by the infpectors to the commiffioners of the county of Philadelphia, who are authorized to, and procure, a reimburfement, by drawing orders upon the treafurer of the county, from which they are removed.

The quantity of ftock and materials, working tools, and implements neceffary for the conftant employment of the prifoners, are purchafed by the jailer, with the approbation of two of the infpectors, and payment for them provided by the commiffioners of the proper county. He delivers out their work, and receives it from them by weight or meafure, as the cafe might be, in order to prevent embezzlement and wafte. The work affigned the prifoners is adapted to

— their

their age, fex, and circumftances of health or ability, regard being had at the fame time to the employment which is moft profitable.

The agreement for the moft valuable fpecies of labour, fuch as ftone-cutting, and fawing marble, as likewife for the purchafe of nails, is made between the infpector and employer. The contracts for other work, as fpinning, cabinet-makers, or joiners work, &c. are commonly entered into with the jailer.

For each convict, a feparate account is kept by the jailer, charging him with his clothing, fuftenance, &c. and in which a reafonable allowance for his labour is credited. It is generally rather lefs than the wages of other workmen in the city. Thefe accounts are balanced at fhort periods, in order that the overplus or proportion, which might be due to the prifoner, may be paid into the county treafury for fafe keeping ; and, once in every three months, they are audited before the infpectors. The committee of infpectors, once during the fame period of time, fix the charges for the prifoners maintenance, which depend on the exifting price of provifions, &c. It is now one fhilling and three-pence per day for the males, and feven-pence for the females. There are few who do not earn above two fhillings. The marble fawing and manufacturing of nails are the moft lucrative employments followed in the prifon. Several were pointed out to us, who earned at thefe occupations above a dollar, and one in particular, whofe daily labour averaged one dollar and an half.

The clothing of the convicts is altogether manufactured in the prifon, and adapted to the climate and feafon. In winter, the men are dreffed in jackets, waiftcoats and trowfers of woollen ; and in fummer, with coarfe linen fhirts and trowfers. The women in plain gowns of the fame. The ftuff for the whole is woven by the males, and made up by the females. There is, at the fame time, not a mattrefs, fheet, rug,

coverlid,

coverlid, nor any thing elfe in that line, but what is likewife manufactured in the houfe. The ftore-room contained a great ftock, and variety of articles, in quality equal to any thing of the kind I have feen for fome time. The moft valuable articles, fuch as nails, plaifter of Paris, marble, &c. are in fuch de- mand, as generally to be difpofed of as foon as manufactured or prepared.

Great attention is paid to the health of the prifoners. On any perfon's complaining, and upon examination of the phyfician found to be difeafed, he is removed to the infirmary of the prifon, his name entered on a book kept for the purpofe, and there remains until he is in a proper condition to leave it. The time is determined by the report of the phyfician, which, as foon as made, is entered in the keeper's book, when the prifoner muft immediately refume his accuftomed employment.

While at their work, the prifoners are permitted no finging or laughing, nor indeed any converfation, exceptfuch as may immediately relate to their bufinefs. This prohibition of all unneceffary converfe is relied upon, as an effential point for the complete admini- ftration of the prifon; and whoever will fubfcribe to the doctrine, that the lefs exertion which is given to the nerves and organs of fenfe, muft calm the ftate of the fyftem, and, by an immediate confequence, foften the difpofition of the heart, will as readily confent to the policy of the regulation. But, to enter a jail, you will fay, without being importuned by the frequent and infolent requefts of fome prifoners, or alarmed for your fafety, from the daring threats and villainous miens of others, can alone proceed from the moft extraordinary and fevere difcipline : and yet in this prifon it is effected with eafe.

This filence, which the infpectors have been fo ftrict in enjoining upon the labourers, has been as rigidly put in practice, and is the firft circumftance that

that will arreſt the attention of a ſtranger. The behaviour and looks of the criminals, at the ſame time, do not border on diſguſt, and of courſe not troubleſome, as on no account are they permitted to addreſs, or beg alms of a viſiter—nor do they do it. Having been left alone with the priſoners, at different times, in their ſeveral apartments, we wanted not opportunities to diſcover, whether the fear of their keepers, or their own conviction of the neceſſity of the regulation, had the greateſt weight in reſtraining them from a breach of it : the latter we found to predominate. None of them ever made the firſt advances to converſe with us, and only once was a requeſt ventured, and then by an induſtrious ſhoemaker—and for what think you ?—For a piece of tobacco.—Fortunately one of our company had a little, which was given him. A chew of tobacco is eſteemed a luxury with moſt of them, but ſtrongly forbidden by the inſpectors, and perhaps with much reaſon. It is an idle, dirty habit, affords no nutriment to the body, and not unfrequently leads to intemperance in drinking. However contrary our gift was to the rules of the priſon, and notwithſtanding it might have given offence, had it been known, ſtill we ſhould never reproach ourſelves with our conduct. He muſt want a heart indeed, who could not have found a diſpoſition to relieve, if placed in a ſimilar ſituation. The man was induſtrious, his air intereſting, the manner of his requeſt modeſt and becoming.

All the priſoners riſe at the dawn of day ; ſo that after making their beds, cleanſing and waſhing themſelves, and other little neceſſary arrangements, they generally commence their labour by ſun-riſe. After this no convict can go into any part of the houſe, other than the place or apartment aſſigned for his buſineſs ; and particularly the nailers, carpenters, ſhoemakers, and weavers, who can, on no pretence whatever, leave their ſhops, or permit any other

priſoner

prifoner to come into them, without giving immediate information to their keeper, or by permiffion of the keeper. The rooms in which they work are not locked. About feven are in a fhop, one of whom is appointed by the jailer, whofe duty it is ftrictly to notice all offences, and in default of it, is punifhed according to the rules. For this, however, there is little or no neceffity, as they commonly work under the mutual infpection of each other. The keepers conftantly parade among the prifoners, in the court-yards and paffages.

At the approach of dufk the bell is rung, when they muft leave off labour, immediately repair to their rooms, and form themfelves in fuch a manner, that the keeper may have a perfect view of every perfon belonging to each room. They remain thus formed, till he calls the roll, and counts them : he then locks them up in their apartments, but without candle or fire, except in extreme cold weather. From this time half an hour is allowed them to adjuft their bedding, after which they are not permitted to con-verfe aloud, or make a noife.

Four watchmen are obliged to continue in the prifon all night : two are within the iron-grated door, and two in the infpector's room. In their turns they patrole the paffages conftantly, and ftrike the bell every hour. They report, on the morning of the fucceeding day, any remarkable occurrence of the night, to the clerk of the prifon, who commits the fame to writing, and lays it before the infpectors at their next meeting.

In going through this prifon, you are not difgufted with thofe fcenes of filth and mifery, which generally diftinguifh jails from other places. On the contrary, the induftry, cheerfulnefs, and cleanlinefs, which meet the eye in every direction, cannot but be peculiarly gratifying. I affure you that my noftrils were not once invaded by the leaft unwholefome or even
offenfive

offenfive fmell. In the bed-rooms, the beds were all made up, and the floors white, and perfectly free from dirt. This was fo furprifing, that one of our company in amazement inquired, how it was poffible to enforce a regulation of this kind among fo many people. " Oh, Sir," anfwered the keeper, " our " method is one and invariable. The prifoners well " know that a tranfgreffion of the rules is never " overlooked, and contrive to adjuft their conduct " accordingly." On converfing further with him, I found that the criminals in the different rooms, for their own convenience and comfort, had adopted among themfelves *fecondary* and inferior governments. One of their principal regulations relative to cleanlinefs was, that no one who found occafion fhould fpit elfewhere than in the chimney. The punifhment annexed to the perfon, who thought proper to infringe this general rule, was fimply an exclufion from the fociety and converfation of his fellow convicts, and this is found to be fufficient.

By the laws of the prifon, the houfe muft be fwept every day by fome one of the convicts. The duty is taken in rotation. It is alfo wafhed once a week in the winter, and twice in the fummer, from one end to the other; and as often in a year completely whitewafhed. A good proof of the cleanlinefs of the place you have, when I mention from authority, that out of eight thoufand and fixty perfons, who were confined in the feveral apartments of the prifon (the debtors jail included) from the twenty-eighth day of September, 1780, to the fifth of the fame month in 1790, only twelve died of natural deaths. Since the latter of thefe periods, the eftablifhment of the new fyftem of difcipline has produced much better arrangements, as well in refpect to the comfort and health, as to the good order and government of the prifoners. This has been evident in feveral inftances. The phyfician's bill, which formerly amounted to

twelve

twelve hundred and eighty dollars a year, feldom exceeds at prefent one hundred and fixty ; and, excepting in cafes of contagious difeafes, not more than two prifoners have died from June, 1791, to March, 1795, a period of nearly four years. During the fall of 1793, when the yellow fever had extended its fatal ravages over every part of the city and fuburbs of Philadelphia, we have from Mr. Carey, in his account of that calamity, that only fix perfons in the prifon were taken fick, and fent to the hofpital; although the fituation of jails, even under the beft adminiftration, makes them moft frequently liable to the generation of contagious and other difeafes. At this time, too, were confined there, by order of the French conful, one hundred and fix French foldiers and failors, befides one hundred other prifoners, compofed of convicts, vagrants, and criminals committed for trial.

What a great object is this, my friend! When we reflect on the poffibility, nay often probability of men being imprifoned for months, and on their trials proving entirely innocent, it certainly fhould be the care of legiflatures, in all countries, to make places of confinement as comfortable as poffible : not to heap fellow citizens together, fubjecting them to all the diforders, which filth and clofenefs of air may occafion. As the temporary forfeit of the liberty of the accufed can only be juftified on principles of neceffity, and as innocence muft be prefumed, until the contrary appears, 'tis unpardonable to add to one mifery, more inconveniences than are neceffary for the fafe keeping of a prifoner. To impofe filthinefs on a convict is cruel; for furely he is fentenced to imprifonment, not to linger out a miferable exiftence by the hand of difeafe. Even the higheft grade of guilt cannot forfeit our compaffion in this refpect towards a criminal, and efpecially when, by withholding it, the community acquires not a fingle advantage.

The

The cleanlinefs of the prifoner's perfon is likewife particularly attended to. On the firft admiffion of a convict, he is feparately lodged, wafhed, and cleanfed, and continues in fuch feparate lodging, till it is deemed prudent to admit him among the other prifoners. The clothes in which he is committed are fumigated and laid by till his difcharge. They regularly fhift their linen, and are fhaved twice a week. Previous to commencing their daily labour, they are made to wafh their face and hands, and in the fummer months, to bathe themfelves in a large bafon in the court-yard provided for the purpofe. Towels are fixed in the different courts. Their hair too is cut decent and fhort once in a month, and for the convenience of the barber, the whole number of men is generally divided into four equal parts; fo that one-fourth part have their hair cut every week.

Independent of the individual comfort naturally arifing from a ftrict attention to cleanlinefs, and its powerful conducivenefs to health, it is more abfolutely neceffary among criminals, than with other perfons. In a prifon government, which contemplates the amendment of its fubjects, it cannot with propriety be neglected. From the connection of the body with the mental and moral faculties, or rather from the influence which the difpofition of the former muft have on that of the latter, it is certain that a man's morals muft, in fome meafure, depend on the proportion of eafe and comfort the body enjoys. Such confidence have the princes and legiflators of ancient eaftern nations placed in this, or fome other like felf-evident propofition, that they conceived cleanlinefs as a very principal phyfical caufe, in correcting the vices of their fubjects. Elfe why do we obferve the many purifications by incenfe, cleanfings, and bathing of the body, fo carefully impreffed upon them as an eftablifhed principle of their religion? Thefe rites were chiefly intended to inculcate morality, as well as to guard

against

againſt interruptions to their health by unclean difeafes. How few men are there who do not feel
moſt difpofed to lazinefs and inactivity (the common
parents of many other vices) with a dirty ſkin and
ſhirt !

We witneſſed a circumſtance, which would not
only excite the aſtoniſhment of all, but muſt imprefs
every vifiter's mind with a favourable opinion of the
adminiſtration of the priſon. It is the humanity of the
keepers to the convicts. The opportunities which
keepers of jails generally have of exerciſing a petty
tyranny and cruelty over the criminals entruſted to
them, and their ufe of thefe opportunities—indeed
the many marks of hard-heartednefs and brutality
which can often be traced in their vifages, as well
as in their actions, had almoſt made it proverbial with
me, that to find fellow-feeling in one of them, *is as
difficult as to difcover crocodiles in Greenland, or fea-
calves in Egypt.* And to be told, that a turnkey was
beloved by criminals, would hitherto have been a
matter of as much furprize to me, and entitled to as
much of my credit, as of *Reynard* being attached to
a hound. Neither of them I conceived to be within
the limits of probability. I have however been dif-
appointed : Yes, my friend,—I *have* been in a priſon,
where the heart of a turnkey is like that of another
man, and where humanity is the ſtanding order of
the day.

It is the chief object of the keepers, to command
as much refpect as poſſible from the criminal, and yet
without laying him under any undue fear or reſtraint.
By thefe means the convict becomes infenfibly and
gradually attached to him, and his mind better prepared to receive any impreſſion he might wiſh to
make. The refult of which is, that a keeper feldom
fpeaks to a prifoner, but what he is anfwered with
refpect and with mildnefs.

In

In paffing among the ftone-cutters, a negro in particular attracted our attention. His countenance be-
fpoke contentment, whilft his eyes expreffed an
anxiety that we fhould addrefs him. I relieved it by
interrogating him, as to the length of time he had
been confined, and how he was pleafed with his condition. His anfwer was, nine months, and to continue three more. That with refpect to living, clothing, and treatment, it would be ingratitude in him
to complain. On afking the caufe of his confinement,
he related to us with the moft interefting eagernefs,
all the circumftances of his commitment and trial,
endeavouring to convince us of his innocence of the
fraud for which he had been condemned. We dif-
fembled, and appeared to be perfectly fatisfied with
his tale, which gave him pleafure. He felt happy
that we fhould depart with a favourable opinion of
him. The cafe was the fame with others whom we
accofted, who appeared delighted at the opportunity
of telling us a favourable tale. Several of the prifoners again held down their eyes, and appeared
affected that we fhould look on confcious folly. But
in the countenances of none did we perceive thofe
marks of hardened villainy and audacioufnefs, which
too unfortunately characterize the inhabitants of
prifons.

Although reformed in other refpects, many of them
perfevere in attefting their innocence, when addreffed
by a ftranger. This diffimulation muft be expected;
for what muft be the fenfations of one of thefe men,
on reading in the vifage of a vifiter, an impreffed
certainty of his guilt. Were he confcious of it, and
had repented of the action, would he not be anxious
to remove it? Yes—nature, in order to pourtray
herfelf in the faireft colours, would often perfuade
a man to encroach thus far upon the laws of morality.

Another incident occurred in our vifit to the women's apartment, which no lefs evinced the good
treatment

treatment thefe people meet with. The keeper who conducted us through this ward, had been abfent for fome time, and had accidently called on a vifit to the prifon. The women were about retiring from their labour; no fooner was the voice of this perfon heard on entering, than it was recollected by a decent looking young woman ftanding in the paffage, and in a moment *Davies* (for that was his name), was whifpered through all the apartments. With the moft heartfelt expreffions of joy, they haftened from their feats to welcome him on his return, and on his part he received them with a mixed fenfe of tender-nefs and fatisfaction. What a feaft would this have been for an Howard's heart! What a field does it not open for the confoling reflections of every phi-lanthropic mind! Humanity muft always be vene-rated, and enfure its juft weight of applaufe; but when we perceive this divine attribute in the turnkey of a prifon, what panegyric can be too great for that man's virtue, who, in fpite of all the tempting allure-ments to which love of power is apt to incline man-kind, would not defcend to tyranny and cruelty, and in defiance of the long eftablifhed *carmen neceffa-rium* of jailers, can boaft of being a protector—an inftructor—not an iron-hearted overfeer! But why fhould this be faid? Why carry wholly to the credit of an individual, a virtue which is infeparably con-nected with, and proceeds, as fhall hereafter appear, from the beauty of the new fyftem of adminiftration? Nay, more; why throw out an expreffion from which an inference might exift, that there is a poffi-bility of oppreffion and injuftice towards the prifoners? Alas! a too long received impreffion of the horrors —the abufes of thofe fepulchres and abodes of hu-man wretchednefs—ftands my apology. I ought to have kept in remembrance, that the prefent *Phila-delphia Prifon*, from the nature of its inftitution, forbids the very thought.

The'e

Thefe incidents, however, have been mentioned
to fhew that the prifoners are fatisfied and live well ;
and the fact is, they do. The male convicts are
allowed, for breakfaft and fupper, as much as they
can eat of a pudding made of the meal of maize corn,
called mufh *. At dinner they have, three days in the
week, about half a pound of bread, with a pint of
potatoes ; on other days mufh and potatoes : on
Sunday, a pound of wholefome meat is diftributed to
each prifoner. Thofe among them who behave
themfelves well are, at times, permitted the indul-
gence of procuring other provifions, at their own
expenfe, but the practice is not common. The nou-
rifhment of the women is of the fame quality with
that of the males, only not as confiderable, from
their fervices being lefs laborious. Contracts for the
food of all the prifoners are entered into by the
jailer, and the whole paid for by the infpectors.

The drink of the criminals is molaffes and water ;
fpirituous liquors are forbidden, except for medical
purpofes, prefcribed by the attending phyfician ; and
the perfon who fells, or fuffers them to be introduced,
on any other occafion, fubjects himfelf to a penalty
of five pounds : if an officer of the prifon, difmiffion
from office. The reafon of this rigorous regulation
arifes, in the firft place, from the probability of the
abufe which might be made of the practice, were it
once introduced ; and, in the next place, from the
conviction of the infpectors, that thofe liquors act
not fo powerfully in ftrengthening a body, doomed to
more than ordinary toil and labour, as the effects of
good wholefome water. That whatever cheerfulnefs
or vigour it may produce in a labourer, it is merely
temporary, and like all high ftimulatives, its operations
are no fooner at an end, than the fyftem is left ener-

* Similar to the *hominy* of the Southern States, only not fo
coarfe.

vated

vated and fatigued. Nor are the infpectors governed by lefs reafonable motives in their choice of a cheap diet, and the exclufion of much animal food from the convicts. The citizen who once makes a violation of the family compact has left but a very flender claim on the public attention : the only one, if it may be fo called, is their obligation to reftrict him from further opportunities of incommoding them, by reformation or other means ; at the fame time with the leaft poffible expenfe to themfelves. Happily the regulation fallen upon by the infpectors, with refpect to the fubfiftence of the convicts, has appeared more likely to affift, in arriving at this *defideratum* of prifon governments, than many others through the fame medium of diet, although more economical ; that is to fay, the two ideas of *economy* and *utility* are by it more clofely connected. The mufh, on which thefe people are fed, is the fubftance of the moft wholefome and nourifhing grain we know of; extremely light and more eafily digefted than almoft any other fpecies of food : confequently the more ufeful. To thofe perfons who feel difpofed to doubt the efficacy of aliment on the temper and behaviour of men, I need only remark, that the experience and obfervations of feveral of thofe entrufted with the fuperintendance of the prifon, have led them to conclude it as not a trifling contributer to the good order of the convicts. *Moral*, though not always, is often a confequence of *phyfical* evil ; and as we find from our own experience, that different qualities of meat and drink produce in the mind as many temporary defires, degrees of fournefs, gentlenefs, heavinefs or hilarity, fo it is equally reafonable to prefume, that a long and habitual ufe of a light wholefome nutriment, will keep the difpofition more uniformly kind and ferene.

The convicts are called to their meals by the ringing of a bell. We faw the men fit down to their fupper, and I do not recollect a scene more interesting. At one view we beheld about ninety fellow creatures, formerly loft, as it were, to their country, and the world, now collected into one body, and obferving that air of *compofure* and decency to each other, confequent only from a long and continued practice of moral habits. They were feated agreeably to claffes, or rather, the fhoe-makers, ftone-cutters, nailers, carpenters, and weavers, formed each a diftinct clafs. During the time of eating, we witneffed no laughing, nor even an indecent gefture ; but a perfect and refpectful filence reigned along the benches. They remained feated until all were ready to rife, of which notice was given by the attending keeper. They then immediately repaired to their refpective employments. Their eating-room is the left part of the court of the front ground-floor or half ftory.

About one-eighth of the number of convicts compofe the negroes and mulattoes, between whom and the whites, in this country, are none of thofe fhameful, degrading diftinctions you are daily accuftomed to in the Southern States. Tried with the fame legal folemnities, and by the fame tribunals, they have equal privileges with other condemned criminals. At fupper, I obferved, they were all feated at the fame table, a profpect that afforded, as you might well conceive, no fmall gratification. Like Briffot, I can fay, " It *was* to me an edifying fight—it feemed a " balm to my foul." .

Slavery, my Friend, is approaching to its diffolution very rapidly in Pennfylvania ; and I hope, before long, will receive its final death-blow. Liberty, humanity, and reafon, have already decreed its doom. The hand of univerfal juftice is uplifted to inflict it— GOD grant it may fall with vigor !—Slavery in its fulleft extent, however, never was fo perfect as it is in the Carolinas and Georgia. The Africans always poffeffed, in common with other men, the liberty of
life,

life, and other privileges which have been uniformly
denied them in thofe countries. At prefent it can
only exift for a certain term of years, till the flave is
of age, during which time he is placed upon the fame
footing with an indentured fervant. What portion of
rights this clafs of the community at this moment
poffefs, the board of infpectors are extremely careful
and jealous of; fo much fo, that they direct the
vifiting infpectors conftantly to bear in mind, that all
men are free until legal proof is made to the contrary.
They therefore take care that no perfon is held in
confinement on a mere fufpicion of being a runaway
flave ; and thofe perfons who are actually flaves, and
not applied for by proper claims within a limited time,
they return to the fupreme or other court for a
Habeas Corpus, to remove them according to law.

May the fame fpirit of philanthropy, now about to
crufh in this part of the world, every veftige of the
moft difgraceful and inhuman policy that ever exifted
among mankind, extend itfelf at leaft fo far amongft
you, as to procure from your government an amelioration (if nothing more) of the condition of thefe long
injured, thefe cruelly oppreffed people. Shame !
fhame ! to Carolina, that as yet it has not taken place !
How much more edifying to yourfelves and pofterity—
more congenial with your true interefts—more confiftent with the glorious principles, whofe eftablifhment you have affifted in fealing with your blood—
and lefs derogatory to your national character as men,
moralifts, and Americans, would that line of conduct
be, which evinced fome little difpofition to promote
the *gradual* abolition of flavery—An evil univerfally
acknowledged, and no where fo much as among
yourfelves. Let me hope, however, that the impu-
tation of your want of humanity in this inftance will
foon ceafe to have exiftence : that the fordid views of
all *importation-wifhers* may meet with the confufion
they merit. I defpair not that they will—The prompt,

C   the

the friendly relief, always offered to foreigners, whom reverfe of fortune and other miferies of war have caft on your fhores ; your no lefs benevolent attention to the diftreffes of your own citizens ; your noted hofpitality to all ftrangers and travellers, all, all confpire to perfuade me, that Carolinians muft, in the natural courfe of affairs, and, before long, be as ftrongly chara&terized for their juftice and fellow-feeling to thofe more immediately around them at home.— Gratitude for favours fecures an intereft in the heart. Revenge is often the only confolation to a mind in chains.

To return from this digreffion. A perfon would conclude, that among thefe prifoners, made up of the dregs of fociety, there could not poffibly exift the harmony and good order which pervades and is vifible in every part of the prifon, and naturally inquire, by what means this decency of deportment can be brought about. I will anfwer you, my dear Sir : not by fuch corporal punifhment as whipping. This is now entirely unknown in the prifon : the keepers are not even allowed to lay violent hands on any of the criminals. I have often wondered, for my part, that, in civilized countries, fuch a mode of punifhment fhould be countenanced—one that originated among favages. To expofe the bare back of a human creature to the lafh of a whip, or cow-fkin, is, to me, horrid : I never faw it executed, without feeling every fenfe of indignation. It is furely from a principle of barbarity that a government infli&ts this punifhment ; for it is pra&tifed among fo many enlightened nations, that candour would forbid the attributing it to their ignorance of its inutility. Can it be fuppofed, that, after fixing upon a man fo indelible a ftigma as the furrows of the lafh, any hope of reformation can be cherifhed ? Is not all his fpirit deftroyed, while labouring under an infamy of the kind ? And will it not finally force him to defpair,

and

and confequently oblige him to feek revenge, by
repeatedly harraffing the race who occafioned it?—
Where, I afk, is the victim to the fcourge, who has
not become more hardened and depraved? Alas!
fad experience anfwers, None! An inftance can
fcarcely be adduced of a criminal being thoroughly
reformed by whipping. The amendment, if any,
has been at moft only temporary: juft as when the
foldier, who has been more than once brought to the
halberd, will, while in the ranks, obey his com-
mander, and do his duty; but is no fooner difcharged, than he is ripe for plunder on the fociety
with whom he is garrifoned.

Befides, the flighteft examination into the fprings
of human action will fully demonftrate the ufeleffnefs
of this mode of punifhment. We know that there
are in every man, even in the moft hardened offenders, fome few fparks of honour, a certain confciouf-
nefs of the intrinfic beauty of moral goodnefs, which
though they may be latent and apparently extinguifh-
ed, yet may at any time be kindled and roufed into
action, by the application of a proper ftimulus. This
ftimulus muft not be fuch a one as would, in its
operations, fupprefs any of thofe paffions with which
it ought to act in unifon; but, on the contrary,
fhould awaken them as much as poffible. A very
predominant one is emulation: deftroy that, and you
at once paralyze the efforts of the foul, and place the
axe to the root of all that is good and great. It is
this paffion which fpurs us to every worthy action;
governs all ranks, from the prince to the peafant;
and to which we are indebted for a great part of the
improvements which have taken place among mankind. Were it not for this, there would be little
inducement for the moralift to point out the relative
duties of man, confidered as a member of fociety;
or the philofopher to engage in his arduous refearches
into the unexplored principles of nature. Both pro-

ceed

ceed from a hope of reward, or profpect of good : for, as the former is actuated to the practice of a virtue, becaufe it is fo highly appreciated by his Maker, fo the latter is anxious to be foremoft in his difcoveries for the utility of the world.

Emulation, then, being a principal, and often an only incentive to a moral conduct, it is evident that the punifhment of whipping, which tends to ftifle it, is an improper ftimulus, and muft neceffarily involve in its confequences nothing beneficial ; while it cannot fail, at the fame time, to reduce a man to the pitiable level of a human being, difarmed of one of the moft amiable paffions. And what is he in this fituation ?— A mere machine, moved at pleafure, by every ftroke of the cat.—His labour, it is true, may be produced by it, for there is no warring againft bodily pains ; but this is the leaft which is required : one of the principal ends of punifhment, the amendment of the offender, is defeated, and irrecoverably loft.

Howard feems to have thought, that whipping was at times abfolutely neceffary in the management of fome criminals, and mentions in his works, I think, an inftance or two of its good effects. With the greateft deference to fo fuperior a judgment, I can never fubfcribe to this opinion, for the reafons juft mentioned. With children or boys, no other principle than that of fear will govern, and perhaps no punifhment avail more than whipping : but where reflection once holds a poft in the mind, I have been always firmly perfuaded, that mankind would more likely be reformed by almoft any other mode, than by a feverity of this kind. A profligate fon we find may be generally amended by precepts given in the influxious language of parental inftruction, and why defpair of the fame remedy to overcome the vices of a criminal—A nation is merely a family in large. But let us look into, and examine the human heart, for the truth of this affertion, and what room is there

for

for doubt? Do we not perceive its natural difpofition fuch as ftubbornly to oppofe the moft approved precepts, when an adherence to them is demanded with the rude commands of tyrannical authority, or attempted to be enforced by a punifhment like this. On the contrary, how yielding is it to the calm and foothing voice of perfuafion or reflection!

The managers of the prifon have fo great a confidence in the efficacy of mild and gentle meafures of treatment, that they will not fuffer, on any account, fuch a conftraintive meafure as placing a criminal in irons; conceiving it by no means calculated to produce in the mind of the convict, the amelioration which is thought fo effential for his amendment. Nor are the keepers permitted to carry fabres, piftols, or weapons of any kind, as is cuftomary in prifons, nor even a cane, for fear that on a trifling provocation they might be induced to beat a criminal.

The keepers and turnkeys, my dear Sir, are not fimilar in any refpect to thofe in other countries; for independent of the little inclination they might have to ill treat a criminal, the ftrong recommendations required for their fobriety and humanity, being always neceffary to the appointment of proper perfons to fill thofe offices, ftill they would find the abufe almoft impracticable, from the unremitted vigilance and attention of the infpectors. The appointment too of the jailer is more particularly attended to, as upon him, in a great meafure, devolves a duty, which, if well executed, cannot fail to enfure a more complete fuccefs to the new mode of difcipline. His falary, therefore, is fully adequate to his fervices, as are thofe of the inferior officers. The total prohibition again of all perquifites, whether arifing from the purchafe of favours, or the retailing of fpirituous liquors, difmiffion fees, and in fact extortions of any kind—the unqualified profcription of fetters, beating, and all arbitrary conduct whatever—

ever—and the end of the inftitution, aiming at the reformation inftead of the debafement of criminals, makes the jailer's duty an humane one, and of courfe renders the place an object with many worthy perfons in the community; when in moft parts of the world, the nature of their prifon governments partakes of fo much depravity, that the very exiftence of them depends on the exclufion of men of fenfibility from thofe ftations. The immediate adminiftration then of the prifon, being in the hands of officers of this oppofite defcription, the amendment of the prifoner, and the example given to fociety, by his fevere yet juft and humane punifhment, can be accomplifhed by few. or perhaps no better regulations than what have been adopted.

On the firft entrance of a convict, the infpectors receive from a proper officer of the court, before whom the conviction was had, a brief report of the circumftances attending his crime; particularly fuch as tend to palliate or aggravate it, with other information refpecting his behaviour on his trial, and his general conduct previous to and after receiving the fentence of the court. This knowledge of the prifoner's character and difpofition, while it affords them an opportunity of afcertaining the degree of care, which may be requifite for the annihilation of his former bad habits, is yet attended with another advantage, that it early evinces to the criminal the ftrictnefs with which he may afterwards expect to be treated. He is then informed of and made fully acquainted with the rules and government of the prifon, and at the fame inftant no pains are wanting, on the part of the infpectors, to enforce upon his mind the ftrength of moral obligations—the breach he has made of thofe obligations—the confequent injury done thereby to the fociety which protected him—the forfeit he has made of that protection—and the neceffity of making a compenfation by his example

or

or amendment. Add to this, every encouragement is given him to perform his duty with alacrity, and to obferve a decency of conduct towards his keeper and co-affociates. Animated alfo with a promife and hope, that an enlargement before the expiration of the term he is fentenced to, will moft probably follow a long and uninterrupted line of good behaviour, the prifoner eafily becomes fenfible of the policy of a refpectful, induftrious deportment.

The infpectors, it ought to have been mentioned, are authorized to intercede with the executive power for the pardon of reformed convicts, and are generally able by their influence to obtain it. The right neverthelefs they never exercife, but with extreme caution, and unlefs, from the repeated reports of the jailer and keepers, they are perfuaded that a prifoner has uniformly demeaned himfelf with propriety, has repented of his paft follies, and in fact that a vifible change and complete amendment has taken place.

At times the infpectors, in their tour of duty, make it a point to difcourfe with all the criminals, one by one feparately, in order to affure them of their relative duties, confidered as men, moralifts, and members of fociety. The exhortations, on thefe occafions, proceed from them with fuch a philanthropic calmnefs, fo much warmth of heart, that their appearance among the convicts never fails to caft a frefh beam of comfort on every countenance. Richard H. M*****, Efq. entered while we were in the women's ward. He had the jail book in one hand, and a pencil in the other. This is cuftomary with the infpectors on duty. Among others, a young negrefs accofted him on the fubject of her confinement. With fimplicity was her tale delivered—with attention was it liftened to. Her fentence, if I miftake not, was two years imprifonment, nine months only of which had been complied with. No exception was ever taken to her conduct fince her firft entrance; it had been regularly pleafing. But the

the demand for a difcharge was certainly unreafonable, and in that light viewed by Mr. M. and all of us. On his expoftulating with her, on the impropriety of remitting fo great a proportion of the fentence, fhe declared herfelf fatisfied with his reafoning, and refumed her employment at the fpinning-wheel with cheerfulnefs and activity.——Such, my friend, is the refult of deliberate perfuafion in matters of this kind.

A criminal again, is well aware that wantonly to infult, or thwart the precepts of an infpector, would, in addition to the penalties annexed to this tranfgreffion by the rules of the houfe, render him defpicable in the eyes of his brother convicts—a confideration of ferious weight with all of them. But laying this entirely afide, we might venture to predict that nothing of the kind would probably take place. For where is the wretch fo bold in iniquity, fo debafed and void of fenfibility, who would delight in ruffling the feelings of one, whofe only incentive to the tafk of fuperintendance is his difpofition to footh the unfortunate—to feek them in their mifery—and pour into their fouls the healing draught of confolation? Say not among criminals, or any other clafs of men. An experiment has been made no where excepting in Pennfylvania. Even under the beft adminiftrations abroad, where prifoners are carefully and well treated, they have notwithftanding been more or lefs influenced by a belief, that their good fortune proceeded rather from oftentatious, or other motives of their benefactors, than any real fympathy for their condition. That with all the humanity of their governors, they can ftill difcover in their conduct fomething like an inward contempt for them. This, no doubt, will always remain a formidable bar to their amendment; and to remove it, it is barely neceffary to affure thefe people, by actions or other means, that you attribute their fituation to misfortune, to bad education, and other adventitious circumftances in life—not to any

innate

innate thirſt for vice or villany. That knowing their
faults and errors, you would ſooner conceal them in
the unfathomable depths of oblivion, than merely
cover them with the ſlight veil of a counterfeited
friendſhip : all which are actually enjoined on the
inſpectors, by the powerful dictates both of duty and
inclination.

All means are uſed by the inſpectors to promote
moral and religious improvement in the priſon, by
the introduction of uſeful books amongſt thoſe who
requeſt them, and the procuring the regular performance of divine ſervice. To aſſiſt them in the
purſuit of the latter arrangement, the taſk is voluntarily undertaken every Sunday forenoon and after-
noon, by ſome one of the ſociety of Friends *, or the
clergy of different denominations, and ſometimes by
the biſhop. The ſervice conſiſts of a ſermon, and a
lecture, on ſubjects ſuited to the ſituation of the con
victs. All the convicts, and other priſoners, both
male and female, are compelled to give attendance,
and arrange themſelves according to claſſes. This is
the only time in the week that the different claſſes of
priſoners have a view of each other. From one of
the inſpectors I learned, that their attention to the
ſpeaker, and decency of conduct, on theſe occaſions,
is peculiarly ſtriking to a by-ſtander. The place appointed for the purpoſe is the long court of the firſt
front ſtory.

After ſo many different methods of inculcating
morality among the inhabitants of the jail, a very
ſtrong motive to the effecting of which is found to
be the good example and reformation of the major
part of them, you may inquire, Are there not men,
nevertheleſs, ſo hardened as to require a much more
forcible reſtraint from vice than this ? Is there no
motive of fear to govern characters like theſe ? No

* Quakers.

puniſhment ?—

punifhment ?—Yes, my friend—there is a principle not only of fear, but of horror—there is a dreaded punifhment, as fhall be explained to you.

When a convict has committed an offence, by re-fufing to labour, by profane curfing and fwearing, or by quarrelling and abufive words, &c. he is firft warned of it by the infpectors, the jailer, or the keeper, but no harfh words are fpoken by either of them, to damp the fpirit of, or expofe the prifoners. On the contrary, I repeat, that every mild meafure is made ufe of to perfuade them from the fame error, and how much it is their intereft to adhere to an uniform good behaviour. If this fails in bringing a criminal to a proper fenfe of his mifconduct, and he is obferved to be ftill callous, and likely to continue fo, recourfe is finally had to a punifhment, which places him in a fituation where nothing but reflection can occupy his mind, and which muft neceffarily compel him to liften to the advice of another monitor. This is by folitary confinement, which leads me to defcribe you the cells which we laft of all vifited.

Thefe cells are contained in a brick building of two ftories, raifed upon arches, and early directed by the legiflature to be built, for the purpofe of this mode of punifhment. It is contiguous to the eaft wing of the prifon, and fituated in a yard of the dimenfions of one hundred and eighty feet by feventy. The greateft part of the yard is appropriated for a garden, managed by fome of the convicts, wherein are a variety of fruits and vegetables. In number the cells are fixteen, and from their peculiar con-ftruction and folitary fituation, appear to me to be better calculated to bring an offender to a review of himfelf and conduct, than any punifhment that can poffibly be contrived. The dimenfions of them are eight feet in length, fix in breadth, and ten in height, with no ground floor, ftrong thick partition walls and arched over with brick. They are all
ranged

ranged along paſſages five feet wide, in the firſt and
ſecond ſtories of the building. The entrance at the
head of each ſtair-caſe is well ſecured, by a ſtrong
door with locks and bolts, and the entry to each
paſſage with two other doors, one of wood, faſtened
by a chain to another of iron. To each cell, again,
there is a wooden and iron door, the latter ſecured
by a long bar fitting a ſtaple in the wall, about two
feet from the door and faſtened, ſome of them with
padlocks, and others by bars running through the
ſtaples down to the floor. In every cell there is one
ſmall window, placed high up and out of the reach of
the convict; the window well ſecured by a double
iron grating, ſo that, provided an effort to get to it
was ſucceſsful, the perſon could perceive neither
heaven or earth, on account of the thickneſs of the
wall, and a *louver* outſide admitting the light in an
oblique direction from above. The criminal, while
confined here, is permitted no convenience of bench,
table, or even bed, or any thing elſe but what is
barely neceſſary to ſupport life, without a riſk of
endangering his health. A privy is placed at one
corner of his apartment, leading to the common ſewer
communicating with the river, which may be cleanſed
at pleaſure by turning a cock fixed to a pipe: this
pipe is conveyed to a ciſtern, placed in the upper
part of the building, near the roof, filled with water
by a pump deſcending through the entries of each
ſtory to a well under the building. The ſituation of
theſe cells is high and healthy, not ſubject to damps,
as dungeons under ground generally are. They are
finiſhed with lime and plaiſter; white-waſhed twice a
year; and in every reſpect as clean as any part of the
priſon. In winter, ſtoves are placed in the paſſages,
to keep the cells warm, from which the convicts may
receive a neceſſary degree of heat, without being able
to get at the fire. No communication whatever between the perſons in the different cells can be effected,
the

the walls being fo thick as to render the loudeſt voice perfectly unintelligible ; and as to any other ſound, excepting the keeper's voice, and the unlocking of doors, they feldom hear. That the criminal may be prevented from feeing any perfon as much as poſſible, his proviſions are only brought him once a day, and that in the morning.

You may conceive, my friend, what an effect the puniſhment of being confined in one of theſe cells muſt have on a refractory offender. For, befides every confideration of a dreary folitude and a want of comfort, and which muſt neceſſarily produce in a mind, thus forced to its own meditations, an uneafy remembrance of the convicts crime and errors, there is added a more painful one ; that is, only half an allowance of proviſions, confifting of bread and water. The utility of the puniſhment has been fully demon-ſtrated by experiment ; for a priſoner was feldom known to continue long in a cell, before he has early become fenfible of the difference of his fituation, and would willingly have returned to that regularity of conduct and induſtry, which his mifguided folly had induced him to depart from. Several of the moſt hardened and audacious criminals, on whom all other modes of difcipline were attended with effects the very reverfe of what they were defigned to produce, and who in fact were held as objects incapable of amendment, have been, by the fimple puniſhment of *folitary* confinement, transformed into fuch a calmnefs of difpofition, as to have become entire new beings, and the leaſt troublefome afterwards among the priſoners. We faw three perfons in the cells :— they pleaded hard for their enlargement once more among their fellow convicts, and offered to conform to any labour, to be relealed from their miferable manfions.

As to the quantum of confinement neceſſary to reform a priſoner, it is determined at the difcretion
of

of the jailer, who is notwithſtanding obliged to inform
the inſpectors of it as ſoon as convenient. For a
criminal who refuſes to labour, it is generally forty-
eight hours, and for other offences in a like proportion, according to the exigence of the caſe. It
operates extremely to the prejudice of a convict to
undergo this puniſhment, as he incurs by it a loſs of
the expenſes of his board, waſhing, and lodging,
which are ſtill charged to his debt, and to make up
which muſt conſequently render his induſtry and ſer-
vices the greater after being again employed.

Beſides thoſe ordered into the cells for tranſgreſſing
the rules of the houſe, there are other perſons, whoſe
original ſentence includes the article of ſolitary confinement, as well as hard labour. Theſe are the convicts contemplated by the law as belonging to the firſt
claſs ; ſuch as perſons guilty of rape, arſon, and other
offences, of which I have already ſpoken. They are
not made, however, to undergo the whole of their
term of confinement at firſt, although the greateſt
proportion is generally required, before they are
permitted to labour. The inſpectors have the power
to direct the infliction of it at ſuch intervals, and in
the manner they ſhall judge beſt, provided the whole
term is complied with, during the ſtay of the criminal
in priſon. Perſons of this deſcription and claſs, are
upon their requeſt furniſhed with a book to read,
generally the New Teſtament.

There is not, perhaps, a phyſical cauſe, which has
ſo powerful an influence on the moral faculty, as that
of *ſolitary* confinement ; inaſmuch as it is the only one
which can give a friendly communication with the
heart. We become by it gradually acquainted with
a true knowledge of ourſelves ; with the purity of
the dictates preſcribed to us by our conſciences ; and
of courſe eaſier convinced of the neceſſity of con-
forming to them. It is in this ſtate of ſecluſion from
the world, that the mind can be brought to contem-
plate

plate itfelf—to judge of its powers—and thence to acquire the refolution and energy neceffary to protect its avenues from the intrufion of vicious thoughts ; for " the actions of men are nothing more than their " thoughts brought into fubftance and being." I need not prefs upon you, that thefe unfriendly vifiters are never fo well recommended, as when aided by the difguifes of fociety. They are then too apt to wreft the fceptre from our enthroned reflection, and leave us bereft of its falutary fway. But in what ftate can this guardian of our morals reign with more unin- terrupted tranquillity, than in one where fcarcely a worldly object prefents itfelf to the eye ; or, in other words, where fo uncontrouled as in the cells of the prifon? May we not hence prefume, that the un- ceafing influence of folitude would, in time, eradicate every relict of vice which might be lurking in the inner receffes of the mind? Certainly; and it was the confidence which the infpectors, at a very early period, had in the reafonablenefs of this theory, that induced them to add practice to it—a trial which, as already obferved, has more than anfwered their moft fanguine hopes of its fuccefs.

We completed, by a view of the folitary cells, our whole tour through the prifon. We were an hour going through the different apartments ; and I declare to you, that never did I before vifit a place which gave me as much fatisfaction—never once in a manu- factory, in which induftry and her almoft infeparable companions, good order and contentment, appeared to have fo firm an abode. I had heard much of the place before I went, but confefs it exceeded every idea I had formed of it ; and to convey you the fame perfect idea of the inftitution I have, is not in my power. Suffice it to fay, that our compaffion was appealed to by no diftreffing tale of tyranny, or ill ufage, no cries of poverty, no fighs nor tears of wretchednefs : on the contrary, we witneffed all that
could

could delight and gratify the mind. Cleanlinefs not often equalled, even in private houfes—labour ever fteady and conftant—infpeƈtors inftruƈting—keepers perfuading—and criminals receiving, with attention and thankfulnefs, precepts for their future regulation and conduƈt: in a word, the whole prefenting one piƈturefque fcene of humanity, juftice, benevolence, and gratitude.

On taking our leave, we made offer of a fmall donation, which was refufed with a polite anfwer, that the prifon fupported itfelf—and it does, my friend. Government or the public contribute not one fhilling towards the maintenance of the jailer, keepers, &c. or to the payment of their falaries and other expenfes. The money is fimply advanced by them. For a long time it was a matter of doubt with moft people, many of them friends too to the new code, whether the proceeds of the labour of the conviƈts would ever defray the expenditures of the houfe. Mr. Howard himfelf affures us, that, " however it might appear " in fpeculation, in praƈtice it was always found the " reverfe. That in the beft regulated houfes in " Holland, taxes are fixed for their fupport." From the experience then of this ftate, every encourage-ment is held out to the citizens of South Carolina, to delay no longer their aid to the completion of this grand work of philanthropy. The additional cofts which muft naturally attend, in another country, a reform after the example of Pennfylvania, from building a fuitable jail and penitentiary houfe, would, I am aware, prefent itfelf to numbers as an obftacle of moment, and no doubt has already had an influence on the minds of fuch part of the legiflatures of other ftates, as at prefent feem but *half* difpofed for an alteration in their criminal codes. But this confide-ration ought to yield to another more weighty. The expenfe can at all events be only temporary, and would be far lefs to the government in the refult.

By

By the books and accounts of the Philadelphia prifon
it appears, that the yearly aggregate of the difburfe-
ments has not, for feveral years paft, amounted to as
much as it did formerly; notwithftanding the alteration made in the modes of punifhment throughout the
ftate has rendered it expedient to maintain more perfons in confinement, and for longer periods. For this
reafon, under the prefent difcipline, prifoners are not
governed by beating, by irons, or any capricious con-
ftraints of turnkeys. Convicts, vagabonds, perfons
accufed, unruly, or runaway apprentices, or fervants,
are not now intermingled and heaped together. Lenity
has fuperfeded the abufe of power; cleanlinefs and
comfort take the place of filth and mifery. Hence
not as many difeafes, quarrels, or efcapes—a neceffity
for fewer keepers—lefs medical affiftance, carpenters,
or blackfmiths repairs, &c. The phyfician's bill
actually does not amount to the fame by four-fifths;
that of the blackfmith has decreafed in a ftill greater
proportion. So that this annual overplus expected
to arife from the greater economy of one fyftem than
the other, would of itfelf foon form a fund adequate
to the reimburfement of fuch fums as might be neceffarily advanced for the purpofe of commencing a reform; while the iffues and profits of the different
eftablifhments of manufactories by the labour of
criminals, would afford a clear and confiderable gain
to the government. But even fuppofing, for inftance,
that the whole would occafion an increafe of the
public taxes, what is it, when placed in competition
with the numerous advantages that may follow—the
peace of fociety—the better fecurity of the lives and
property of the perfons upon whom thofe tributes are
levied. No orderly citizen would think his mite ill
beftowed for purpofes of this kind. Legiflatures, at
every feffion, employ themfelves in enacting laws for
cutting new roads, beautifying cities or buildings, and
public money expended to accomplifh them; while
criminal

(45)

criminal codes lay in the archives of a state, and few are induced to revise them, until the parchments on which they are written become either musty or worm-eaten. At the same time, there offers no where a more ample field for improvement than in the science of forming good penal systems; for of all others it has, in proportion to its magnitude, been the least attended to: and surely few ought to be more interesting, as few are more immediately connected with our happiness. The chief end of civil government is a preservation of the social compact; and as public measures approach to that point, so must they preserve a greater degree of brilliancy, and become more the objects of general admiration.

To return, however. The prison and its several apartments are under the superintendance of a board or committee of inspectors, with legal powers, chosen from the mass of citizens. The election of one half of them takes place every six months, when those who desire it are generally re-elected. The appointment rests strictly with the mayor and two aldermen of Philadelphia, and the person chosen cannot decline without incurring a penalty of ten pounds; but the common practice latterly has been, that the inspectors going out of office should nominate as their successors, other persons willing to undertake the duty, which is always confirmed. The board consists of twelve, seven of whom form a *quorum*, and meet once a fortnight in the inspectors' room. Two of them are obliged to go over the whole prison together every Monday, and oftener, if occasion requires, who are named *visiting* inspectors. Their duty is to inspect not only the jailer and other officers, but particularly the behaviour and disposition of the prisoners; to see that they are properly and sufficiently employed; to inquire into their health, and take care that their food is served in quantity and quality agreeably to the directions of the board; that the sick are properly provided for; and

D   that

that suitable clothing and bedding be furnished to all. They hear the grievances of the prisoners, and bring forward the cases of such whose conduct and circumstances may appear to merit the attention of the board. They cause returns to be made out by the clerk of the prison, and laid before the committee monthly, of all the prisoners—their crimes—length of confinement—by whom committed—and how discharged since the preceding return. Besides a regular attendance of the *visiting* inspectors, the prison is every day visited by some one or more of the committee. They all take great delight in, and are indefatigable in the execution of the humane task allotted them.

Subject to the directions of the committee are a jaileress, four keepers, one turnkey, and a clerk. The cook, scullion, barber, and other attendants, are convicts, who are credited for their services in proportion to the time and labour they expend. I was surprised to find a female in the first appointment; and, on inquiry, found that her husband was formerly jailer. Discharging the duties of a tender parent towards his daughter, infected with the yellow fever in 1793, he caught the disorder, and died, leaving the prisoners to regret the loss of a friend and protector, and the community that of a valuable citizen. In consideration of his faithful performance of the functions of his office, his widow was nominated to succeed him. She is exceedingly attentive and humane. Your uncle related to me, what to many would appear a curious anecdote of this lady. It occurred in his visit to the prison. After conversing with her for some time, he inquired of her, whether there were no inconveniencies attending the institution. With the greatest concern she replied, that there was one, which gave her no small degree of uneasiness : that the debtors in their apartments, from being able to overlook the yard of the prison, made her fear that their conversing together, swearing, &c. might corrupt the *morals* of her people.

people. You may think it ftrange, that debtors fhould corrupt criminals ; but the cafe is really fo, for there is certainly as much if not more morality among the latter than the former. And fo fully convinced were the infpectors of her apprehenfions being well founded, that, to remedy the defect, they have fince had the prifon wall raifed.

Purfuant to the directions of the legiflature, the prifon is, at ftated periods, vifited by a committee, confifting of the mayor and a certain number of aldermen, with fome of the judges of the fupreme court. The governor of the ftate likewife, the judges and juries of all other courts, pay a vifit to the infti- tution during the fame intervals of time. Thefe vifits were originally intended by the legiflature, as well in order to afcertain how far the abolition of the old criminal code would be productive of the means of preventing wickednefs and crimes, as to take care that the attention of the infpectors fhould be unre- mitted. They are now rendered not fo neceffary, as the innovation has been crowned with fuccefs, and the vigilance of the infpectors not likely to diminifh, when none are appointed except upon their requeft or confent. They neverthelefs anfwer one good end ; for the approbation of fuch refpectable committees muft at all times tend to increafe the care of thofe entrufted with the management of the houfe.

There are likewife two other vifiting committees, who do not fuperintend, but notwithftanding have, at any time, from the nature of their duties, free accefs to the prifon. One is from the fociety for alleviating the miferies of public prifons, who, as before obferved, were the chief promoters of the prefent improvement in the penal code. They only pay attention to that part of the prifon where the vagrants and perfons confined for trial are lodged, and to whom feveral of the foregoing falutary regulations do not extend. They afford relief to fuffering prifoners, which they

have

have been able to accomplish to a confiderable extent; partly by means of the annual contributions of the members, and partly by directing the diftribution of what is occafionally given in donations. They pay off fmall fees when the cafe feems to deferve it, and when the party would perhaps be detained for them in confinement: they alfo make applications to the magiftracy for the enlargement of perfons illegally confined, which has fometimes happened from the obfcurity and friendlefs condition of the parties. The other committee comes from "the fociety for the " gradual abolition of flavery," who inquire into the circumftances of every African, or other perfon of colour, and take care that none are imprifoned illegally. The fervices of this committee, in putting a ftop to various acts of oppreffion and injuftice, which otherwife would have taken place either from the tyranny or caprice of *men-holders*, do them infinite honour. No doubt their zeal will increafe with their fuccefs.

The confequences, I repeat, which have marked the progrefs of the lateft legiflative amendments to the criminal laws, have been fo favourable, that crimes have actually diminifhed confiderably, as will appear by the annexed tables. The prefent fyftem too is confidered by its friends as ftill in its infancy. Its effects alfo on the morals of the prifoners have been no lefs evident. Re-convictions are feldom heard of. Of all the convicts condemned for thefe five years paft, not above five in a hundred have been known to return; and, to the honour of human nature be it fpoken, that fome of the convicts, at the expiration of their term of confinement, voluntarily * offered themfelves, while the yellow fever raged in Philadelphia, to attend the fick as nurfes at Bufh-hill, and conducted themfelves with fo much fidelity and

---

* Carey's account of the yellow fever.

tendernefs,

tendernefs, as to have had the repeated thanks of the managers. Few have been known to ftay in the prifon the whole of the term to which they were fentenced, the amendment and repentance of many of them being fo vifible to the infpectors as to have had a claim on the governor's clemency. Some have appropriated the proceeds of their labour, while in confinement, to the fupport of their families; and feveral, on leaving the prifon, have received forty or fifty dollars, the overplus of the profits of their labour, and with this capital turned out honeft and induftrious members of fociety.

Thus you obferve, my friend, what a great portion of humanity is interwoven with the juftice contemplated in this fyftem of criminal jurifprudence, and what a happy effect it has produced on the morals of the abandoned part of the people of this country. It would really appear, that the generally adopted mode of exacting the life of a fellow-citizen, for fo many petty mifdemeanors, and even for offences which are politically and not morally wrong, that the object of punifhments was *not* the prevention of crimes; that they were not intended for example; but that different princes and legiflators had in view a gratification of their revenge, and an increafe of the catalogue of offenders. The conclufion might with juftice be drawn (were we not charitably inclined to attribute their conduct more to error than other-wife) by recurring for a moment to the fatal confe-quences which have proceeded from the practice of fanguinary fyftems, and which have been too obvious to efcape general attention. In cafting an eye over the page of hiftory we fhall find, that in proportion as governments have cultivated a difpofition for en-forcing laws, by rigorous and cruel punifhments, in

the

the fame degree have their defigns been fruftrated, by the more repeated breaches of them.

Firft, from a view of the ancients. No laws were more unjuft, or abounded with fo many cruel and immoderate punifhments, as thofe enacted in the reigns of the Roman kings, and alfo thofe contained in the twelve tables of the Decemviri. In no inftance, per- haps, was the depravity of human nature more com- pletely verified, than in the calendar of crimes which diftinguifhed thofe eras. When the Porcian and Valerian laws * were eftablifhed, the punifhment of death was laid afide; the magiftrates were not even allowed to inflict corporal punifhment on a free citizen. The virtue of the Romans at one of thofe periods was fo great, that Livy tells us, " the only punifhment " denounced againft the tranfgreffors of the Valerian " law was, that they fhould be deemed guilty of a " difhoneft action †". It was at thefe periods the republic was in its fplendor, and happy had they been if they had never loft fight of the excellency of that fyftem! Fortunate their lot, if all the attempts, which were afterwards made to bring into repute the former penal code, had been unfuccefsful! But, alas, the reverfe was their fate! The Cornelian, Pompeian, and Julian laws §, effected a melancholy change, by reviving the penalty of death. It was not till then that a humane fyftem received its firft mortal ftab, and the foundation of a code of jurifprudence finifhed, which, even in the greateft fucceffes of the Romans in after ages feemed a canker to their happinefs. Thus be-

---

* The former of thefe laws was made about three centuries before Chrift, by *Porcius Læcas*, firft tribune of the people, and afterwards one of the *Epulones*. The latter derives its name from *Valerius Poplicola*, who paffed it not long after the expulfion of the kings, and was renewed twice; the laft time by Valerius, a defcendant of his, in more diftinct terms than before.

† Book x. Chap. 9.

§ Made by Sylla, Pompey, and Cæfar.

gun,

gun, it daily acquired ftrength, and was fo invigorated in the reigns of Nero, Claudius, Caligula, and moft of the Emperors fubfequent to the time of Auguftus, that the cruelty of punifhments had arrived to an intolerable height—crimes were multiplied almoft beyond former example—the people were obferved to relapfe rapidly into their priftine infamy and weaknefs—and the whole gradually terminated, though fome few temporary checks were given, in the total ruin of the empire.

In more modern times, the effects of cruel punifhments have not been lefs deplorable. In the eaftern world, where the torture of the wheel had univerfally prevailed, till the latter end of the laft century, crimes were evidently more frequent than after the partial abrogation of it; and in thofe countries of Europe, in which this punifhment was till very lately tolerated, we obferved more heinous offences committed, than in thofe where it was unknown. Before the late Guftavus the Third abolifhed torture in Sweden, and fubftituted pecuniary penalties, and mild corporal punifhments, excepting for few of the moft heinous crimes, the times difplayed very ftriking inftances of the impolicy of fevere punifhments. The bars of the criminal courts of that country, it is well known, exhibit a far more favourable complexion now than what they did at the commencement of that prince's adminiftration. Nor did we ever learn, that the fame ftep taken about that time by the government of the prefent difmembered ftate of Poland, had been productive of other than falutary confequences.

The experience of a very populous European nation, the Ruffians, would alone fhew the ufeleffnefs of capital punifhments. In the reign of Peter the Great, the ftatutes of blood were in full force, accompanied with the perpetration of every excefs which fhocks humanity, and continued fo through the reigns of Catharine, Peter the Second, and Anne, till the acceffion of his daughter Elizabeth. This

princefs no fooner repealed them than crimes diminifhed confiderably, and the empire flourifhed. She
governed the Ruffias for twenty years, and effected
fuch a moderation in the penal code, as never to have
put to death a criminal *. Nor has the late Emprefs
Catharine been lefs perfuaded of the fuperior policy
of fending felons flaves to Siberia, to work in the
mines at Nerfhink, by her abolifhing the punifhment
of death in every part of her dominions §. And it is
certain, that in no part of Europe are crimes fo rare
as in the Ruffian empire ‡.

* " L'Empératrice Elizabeth a achevé par la clémence,
" l'ouvrage que fon père commenca par les loix. Cette indul-
" gence a été même pouffée à un point, dont il n'y a point
" d'exemple dans l'hiftoire d'aucun peuple. Elle a promis, que
" pendant fon regne *perfonne ne ferait puni de mort*, et a *tenu* fa
" promeffe. Elle eft la première fouveraine qui ait ainfi refpecté
" la vie des hommes."—*Hift. de Ruffie par Voltaire.*

§ See Tatifchef's tranflation of the " grand inftructions for
" framing a new code of laws for the Ruffian empire."

‡ " Les grandes crimes ont commencé à devenir plus rares
" fous ce regne, où perfonne n'a été puni de mort." *Hift. de
Ruffie par L'Evefque, Tom. V.* The following firft part of an
extract from the journal of a gentleman, who refided fixteen
months in St. Peterfburg, which he was fo obliging as to furnifh
me with, ferves to ftrengthen what *L'Evefque* has advanced :—
" During my ftay here I have heard of few criminals, and not
" one for an atrocious crime. This, I underftand, is peculiar to
" Ruffia, and may be accounted for from the fuppreffion of fan-
" guinary punifhments ; and likewife to the ftrict police adopted
" throughout the empire. The eftablifhment of police officers
" over all parts of the country, and their continual correfpond-
" ence with each other, make it extremely difficult even for a
" debtor to abfcond from his creditors. A criminal is always
" apprehended." All travellers have confented to the fact of
crimes not being near fo frequent, fince the paffing of Elizabeth's edict, as before. Although the celebrated Mr. Coxe dif-
approves of the generally received impreffion, that the Ruffian
code is a politic one, and advocates the neceffity of the punifhment of death, yet he no where denies that crimes have diminifhed.

In

In Holland and the Auſtrian Netherlands, few
atrocious offenders are to be found *. To what better
cauſe can we aſcribe this circumſtance, than to the
generality of crimes being puniſhed by hard labour in
the raſp, ſpinning, and other houſes of correction,
and alſo to the reformation of criminals effected by
the excellent diſcipline obſerved in them?

Dr. Ruſh mentions a remarkable proof of the
impropriety of the puniſhment of death. " The
" Duke of Tuſcany," ſays he, " ſoon after the pub-
" lication of the Marquis of Beccaria's excellent
" treatiſe on this ſubject, aboliſhed death as a pu-
" niſhment for murder. A gentleman, who reſided
" five years at Piſa, informed him, that only five
" murders had been perpetrated in his dominions in
" twenty years. The ſame gentleman added, that
" after his reſidence in Tuſcany he ſpent three months
" in Rome, where death is ſtill the puniſhment for
" murder. During this ſhort period, there were ſixty
" murders committed in the precincts of that city.
" It is remarkable (continues the doctor) that the
" manners, principles, and religion of the inhabitants
" of Tuſcany and Rome are exactly the ſame. The
" abolition of death alone for murder produced this
" difference in the moral characters of the two na-
" tions." This circumſtance I merely inſert in order
to have an opportunity of corroborating it. On con-
verſing with an Engliſh gentleman, brought up at
Leghorn, who had a very general knowledge of the
government and laws of the ſeveral ſtates in Italy, I

* Mr. Howard had certainly acquired, in Holland, more experience and information, to prove the inefficacy of ſeverity in
puniſhments, than in any other country; for " it appears to have
" been his great ſchool, to which he was never wearied in re-
" turning." His works not only ſhew that *heinous* crimes are
very ſeldom committed, but that even *trifling* offences are not near
ſo common, as might be expected from a country of its popula-
tion.

learnt

learnt that the organization of the new code of laws, by the late Grand Duke Leopold, has not only given rife to confiderable improvements in the prifons at Florence, but rendered offences very rare in that and other cities in the Dukedom, when compared with Rome, Genoa, Turin, or Venice *.

As a further proof of the little tendency which fevere laws have in fuppreffing vice and immorality, and in fact of their injurious effects, let us only turn our eyes towards a government in the eaftern hemif- phere, who have long ranked one of the foremoft as advocates for feverity. What have been the con- fequences of a fanguinary fyftem in that country?— Has it been found from experience, that the morals of the vicious clafs of people have amended at all?— Have the ill-judged meafures, I afk, of fo many of her parliaments, in extending death to trivial offences and contempt of the laws operared in the leaft to prevent them?——No,—for the rights of the induf- trious and peaceable proportion of the community, are no where fo frequently interrupted by the indolent or defperate as in England. Although the fecurity of their perfons and property may perhaps be *partially* accomplifhed by dragging fome offenders to juftice, ftill when they reflect on fuch an unneceffary facrifice of their fellow fubjects, they cannot but lament that

* If any credit can be given to the authorities of well-in- formed travellers, the fact of the wholefome effects proceeding from a change of the penal laws of Tufcany, feems to be fuf- ficiently eftablifhed. The intelligent Dr. Moore, fpeaks highly of it in his travels; and no one with more precifion to perfuade than General Lee in his memoirs. " In fhort," fays the latter, after dwelling on its policy, " Tufcany, from being a theatre of " the greateft crimes and villainies of every fpecies, is become " the fafeft and beft ordered ftate of Europe." Thofe who wifh other and conclufive proof, have fimply to refer to the edict of the Grand Duke himfelf, wherein are expreffed in the preamble, and in ftrong terms of conviction, his reafons and motives for continuing a mitigation of punifhments, which he declares to be founded entirely upon his *own experience of its utility.*

a better

a better remedy fhould be unprovided. But how
dreadful the confideration when they perceive the
ftatute book already fwelled to a bulk unknown in
modern hiftory, and the lift of capital offences increafed at every feffion of their legiflature, by new
tranfgreffions made felony without benefit of clergy.
And thefe at this moment amount to upwards of two
hundred.

Need more be faid to corroborate the foregoing,
let us fimply take a view of the American world.
To repeat that crimes are lefs frequent in this country at this period than they were feveral years ago,
and owing entirely to the late legiflative regulations,
is unneceffary, as may be perceived from a view
of the already referred to tables, and from being
within the obfervation of every inhabitant; and to
fay that in no part of the known world are offences
fo feldom committed as in Pennfylvania, in proportion to its cenfus of inhabitants, will be granted by all
ftrangers and foreigners. At the laft court of feffions
for the county of Philadelphia, there was not one
third of the number of criminals I have generally obferved on the Charlefton docket. This is a great
difproportion for a place in which there is a continual
conflux of ftrangers, and a county containing more
than double the number of inhabitants of Charlefton
diftrict. Your late September calendar of delinquents
was enormous. Fifty-fix indictments to be given out
at one court for affaults and batteries, eighty for
beating conftables, befides the long lift of felonies
and larcenies reported by the judges to the governor,
cannot avoid impreffing the minds of the people in
Pennfylvania, with a horrid idea either of your laws
or police. The fault muft exift in one of them, and
from the knowledge and experience I have been able
to collect, would rather attribute it to a defect in
your penal code than to a bad police. Until you
eradicate from it the penalty of death, for fuch a
variety

variety of petty offences, your laws will not be enforced, and the magiſtracy of them leſs reſpected.

In Maſſachuſetts, where for petty offences the puniſhment of death has been changed for conſtant and
hard labour at the nail factory on Caſtle Iſland, they
are not ſo common as in other ſtates where they
adhere to the old ſyſtem. And in Connecticut, crimes
are not very frequently committed, probably owing
to the dreadful idea which perſons have of being ſent
to the mines and works at Simſbury †.

Having now collected from a few references to the
effects produced by ſanguinary codes of laws in different countries, that they have always derogated
from the morals of their inhabitants, let us endeavour
to aſcertain why ſevere puniſhments thus held up by
a government, ſhould be leſs ſucceſsful in preventing
crimes, than thoſe which are mild and moderate.
This there can be no difficulty in doing, if we examine
into the principles which generally deter a worthleſs
individual of ſociety from tranſgreſſing the rights of
another. The moſt forcible which governs him at
this time will be allowed to be the *dread* of puniſhment, not from a divine hand (for a perſon who ſo
far deviates from the paths of rectitude, as to con-
template an act of injuſtice, thinks little of a puniſhment ſo remote as not to take place in this life), but
from the laws of that community, of which he is a
member. That dread however does not ariſe from
any cruelty or other ſeverity of which a penalty may
be compounded, but from a certainty of its being
inflicted, for, " it is the nature of mankind to be
" terrified at the approach of the ſmalleſt inevitable
" evil, whilſt hope, the beſt gift of heaven, hath the
" power of diſpelling the apprehenſion of a greater."
So that when a law is ſevere, the execution of it is
not ſo certain as if it were a mild one. It is indeed

† Vide Maſſachuſett's Magazine for 1792.

an

an undeniable pofition, that if *feverity* blended with a *certainty* of punifhment, were the inevitable confe-quences of a violation of the laws, offences would feldom be perpetrated. But this can rarely happen, from a principle of humanity inherent in the breafts of moft.perfons, which unavoidably directs them to fubmit to an injury, in preference to enforcing a rigorous law. Man being a compaffionate being, will not feel fo difpofed to appeal to his country for juftice, when he is perfuaded it can be obtained on no other terms than a forfeiture of life. He cannot reconcile to himfelf the idea of taking fo active a part againft the dictates of his reafon and confcience; and will thus, from a forbearance of profecution, im-pliedly encourage tranfgreffions which his judgment difowns, merely on account of the unreafonablenefs of their penalties. From this gulph of error has arifen a rock, upon which fo many nations have divided or deftroyed their happinefs, and are ftill ftrangers.to the melancholy caufe. Little did they expect, that while they paid no refpect to *proportioning* the punifhment to the crime, that the difpofition to profecute would become the more cold and indifferent in the injured, and the rights of individuals more opened to invafion from the feeble operation of the arm of juftice. Lefs did they forefee that the hardened criminal, thus taught to regard the extreme feverity of the punifhment to every offence, as a frefh motive for exciting the compaffion of the humane, would with little hefitation commence his depredations anew on fociety, and finally trample with greater fafety on thofe very laws founded on a fyftem which miftaken policy had devifed as the ftrongeft bulwark. Whereas if-punifhments were mild, moderate, and proportional to the damage incurred, the humane would not be fo generally deterred from profecuting. But as long as a penalty is beyond meafure, and evidently carries with it traces of difproportion and injuftice, informa-
tions

tions will not be fo frequent—juries will hefitate to convict without recommending to mercy—judges to condemn—and confequently the very intent of laws defeated, by thefe repeated examples of exemption. The uncertainty of punifhment, then, is the principal danger which nations have to fear. That excellent obfervation of Montefquieu's, " La caufe des " tous les relâchemens vient de *l'impunité* des crimes, " & non de la moderation des peines," alone ought to increafe our caution in not admitting it amongft us—an obfervation that has acquired at this period, it is hoped, all the ftrength of an incontrovertible principle. An hoft of philofophers have already acknowledged its reafonablenefs in theory, and different ages and nations feem to have crowded as it were, to fix it immoveably on the broad bafis of experience. For what occafioned the number of crimes and infolvent debtors at Rome, under the feverity of the twelve tables, but the flattering hopes and examples of impunity * ? What moulded the minds of the Romans for near three centuries afterwards, to a ftate of virtue and happinefs, fcarcely equalled fince in the annals of hiftory? Was it not the certainty of punifhments and mildnefs of their laws? Why again are crimes now lefs common in Tufcany than in other ftates of Italy, unlefs from the number of *fanctuaries*, and " the *eafe with which*

---

* An hiftorian fpeaking of the liberty given to creditors to difmember the body of a debtor, obferves, that " the advocates " for this favage law infifted, that it muft ftrongly operate in " deterring idlenefs and fraud from contracting debts, which " they were unable to difcharge ; but experience would diffipate " this falutary terror by proving, that no creditor could be " found to exact this unprofitable penalty of life or limb. As " the manners of Rome were infenfibly polifhed, the criminal " code of the Decemvirs was abolifhed by the humanity of ac- " cufers, witneffes, and judges, and *impunity* became the confe- " quence of *immoderate* rigour." Gib. Hift. Rife and Fall Rom. Em. 8 vol. page 93.

" *pardons*

" *pardons are obtained* †" in the latter, and the total
abolition of them in the former? To the foregoing
may be added, that in Ruſſia, where offences are
rare, the *certainty* of puniſhment is great ‡ ; while in
no country is the impunity of criminals ſo trifling as
in Pennſylvania §, or ſo notorious as in England ‖.
  On another ground permit me to purſue this ſubject.
A principal object of puniſhment, it has been ſaid, is
to hold out an example to ſociety, in order to deter
others from offending. The taking the life now of
an unfortunate wretch is not ſuch an example, as
would prevent a depraved individual from launching
into the ſame vicious courſe of life, and no perſon can

† Moore's Travels, vol. 4.
‡ " Crimes, I perceive, (ſays a foreigner), do not go unpu-
" niſhed here as in other parts of Europe I have viſited. Par-
" dons are ſeldom or never heard of. A valet de chambre of
" an Italian Ambaſſador having committed an offence laſt
" week, by wounding a Ruſſian (but not without ſome provo-
" cation), it was not till after an uncommon exertion of the
" Ambaſſador's intereſt at court, that a remiſſion of ſuch part
" of the ſentence condemning him to the mines was granted.
" He notwithſtanding had his noſtrils ſlit, and was immediately
" ordered out of the Empreſs's dominions." Continued from
the firſt part of third note, page 70. marked with inverted
commas.
  Mr. Coxe offers us one of the beſt proofs of the certainty of
the laws being enforced, when he gives us to underſtand in the
anſwer of the Empreſs to his ſeventh query, " that criminals
" never receive a mitigation of their ſentences, unleſs upon a
" general or particular amneſty."
  § Formerly the acquittals formed full one half of the perſons
tried—Now they ſcarcely exceed an eighth part.
  ‖ From the tables in Howard's *State of Priſons,* we learn that,
at the different aſſizes within the Oxford circuit, for ſeven years,
from 1764, 690 perſons were tried, and 615 acquitted ; beſides
293 diſcharged by proclamation. Within the home circuit, from
1764 to 1770 incluſive, 159 burnt in the hand, 96 whipped,
and 386 acquitted. In the Norfolk circuit, from 1750 to 1772,
434 condemned to death, and only 117 executed. In the ſame
ſpace of time for the Midland circuit, 518 condemned to death,
and 116 executed. And at the Old Bailey, London, from 1749
to 1771 incluſive, 1121 ſentenced to die, and 678 executed.
                                                    doubt

doubt this who was ever prefent at an execution. The trifling fhare of pain a convict is fenfible of, and the eafe which attends his departure from mortality, is an exhibition not calculated to create more than a temporary degree of awe in a furrounding multitude, and productive of effects too fudden and violent to leave any durable impreffions on their minds. When thefe impreffions again are apt to create in the breaft of a fpectator, any other emotions than thofe of terror and deteftation of the fufferer's offence, the confe-quences are ftill more prejudicial. How often, neverthelefs, do we experience fenfations the very oppofite of thefe? Is there fcarcely an execution, which does not either prompt us to an admiration of the criminal's intrepidity, or excite our compaffion for his diftrefs ; and thus, by affording a fcene of virtue and fenfibility, render us forgetful of the crime which gave birth to it? Above all, how many men are there, who look upon the ceremony of a fcaffold proceffion with all the indignation imaginable! For myfelf I can avow that, on this occafion, the following train of reafoning forces itfelf upon my mind. What means this tumult, that diforders in this manner the peace and happinefs of fociety? What this combination of thoufands—this waging war againft an helplefs indi-vidual? Does the exiftence of one poor delinquent en-danger the fecurity of a government or nation? If fo, alas, my country, how art thou fallen ! Weak in con-dition indeed! Where is thy *boafted ftrength and energy,* thofe expreffions the infant lips of thy citizens have fo often uttered, and to which we would all attend with the fweeteft rapture ? If deprived of it, is it ftill necef-fary that thou fhouldeft in this folemn and open manner, proclaim thy inability to protect, and defend thyfelf? *He has committed a crime,* I might be anfwered ; *the people muft feel the fovereignty of the government and laws.* And can they not accomplifh this except by the perpetration of a crime ? Becaufe they have ag-
gregately

gregately fuſtained, perhaps not much more than a trifling inconvenience, they are, on this account, to ſeek a poſitive injury, by the loſs and murder of a fellow-creature? Muſt private revenge be abhorred, and a public example of it conſidered as a juſt and proper ſpectacle for a populace? Oh Juſtice! Virtue! Why do men perfiſt in miſconſtruing your divine excellencies? When will they learn, that to reverence a right we all claim from nature, is the only policy which can combine with public tranquillity, the ſecurity of individual comfort. I could not deliberately, and in perfect poſſeſſion of my reaſoning faculties, take the life of an individual, for robbing me of a few ſhillings. Morality riſes in ſtern oppoſition to it —the adviſer, which my Maker has mercifully placed in my boſom, threatens judgment on my future happineſs, were I even to harbour a doubt reſpecting it: what, then, muſt I think of the community who can do ſuch an act? Ought they not to be pronounced as *barbarouſly* vindictive? The action which is in itſelf immoral, cannot become leſs ſo in receiving the ſolemn ſanction of a nation; and to detect public vices, we need only keep in remembrance that nations are but powerful individuals, and equally required with them to be juſt and humane. Theſe reflections, my friend, dwell with weight on my mind, and, I believe, equally influence the mind of others. Or whence the reaſon, that the office of jack-ketch, who innocently executes his country's decrees, is held in univerſal and degrading contempt? Why that general readineſs to ſign a petition for a convict's pardon? It is becauſe men conſcientiouſly diſapprove of, and think with horror on, theſe repeated examples of barbarity and injuſtice.

Crimes may be called diforders of a ſtate, perpetrators of them the parts affected, and legiſlatures the preſcribing phyſicians. How ſurpriſing, that no other remedy ſhould be applied to eradicate the complaint

E   than

than an *amputation* of the infected limb! This is furely
not congenial with the practice of the *regular-bred*
gentlemen of the faculty; for we find that, in a
bodily wound or difeafe, this operation is never re-
forted to, except in a cafe of the utmoft neceffity, and
until all other efforts to prevent its contaminating or
injuring the whole fyftem have been rendered abortive.
For a legiflature then to doom to deftruction a criminal, without making *one* fingle exertion to reftore
him to a juft performance of his duties as an individual of fociety, muft appear as prepofterous, ridi-
culous, and cruel, as to deprive the human body of
one of its members, merely becaufe *that* member is
the feat of complaint. And yet we repeatedly hear
this public conduct juftified by fome men, on the principle that criminals *cannot* be reformed, or in words
more emphatic to convey their ideas, *that moft difeafes cannot be cured.* The clofer this pofition is ex-
amined, the ftronger muft we reprobate it, as not
only irrational and pernicious, but extremely weak
in its foundation. I recollected the other day an obfervation of our American Æfculapius*, at the conclufion

* Dr. Rufh. This name is applied to the Doctor, from the
fkill and eminence to which he has arrived in his profeffion, and
from the circumftance of his reviving a fyftem of medicine,
founded on principles reafonable, and at once clear to the mind
that will unfetter itfelf of prejudice. It is not however the doctrine with reafon on its fide, that will always and at firft make
many profelytes; for, notwithftanding the enlightened era in
which we live, the reverfe is daily experienced. Any digreffion from a long trodden path, however it might have in view
the intereft and convenience of mankind, by fimplifying or
throwing light upon a fcience, feldom fails at the fame time to
roufe either the fhort-lived energy of bitter malevolence, or,
what is more provoking, the contemptible oppofition of *confum-
mate* ignorance. So has it been with this refpectable character—
a character whofe fervices may be known by fimply calling to
mind the fall of 1793. When the capital of his country lay
nearly defolated by the unrelenting fury of a peftilence, he
fcorned

clufion of a courfe of lectures to his medical ftudents,
that all difeafes, not including thofe from accidental
or other fudden wounds, might be cured, were it not
for the interpofition of three caufes; and the moft
important of them, he urged, was the neglect or un-
fkilfulnefs of the phyfician. The obfervation now
ftrikes me, as being clearly applicable to public or
moral diforders; for if we only trace the fource of
all corruption and derangement of the focial fyftem,
we fhall perceive that it originates, like moft fimple
difeafes, not from any fudden wound or contufion,
but from a trifling affection, fprung into exiftence
from the neglect of a criminal, and daily matured
by the ftill greater neglect or ignorance of governments. The moft enlightened ftate phyficians have
not yet been able to preferve, in this refpect, a perfect national health. No wonder, when they have
been fo long and erroneoufly taught to defpair, in
every cafe of mental depravity.

The conduct, again, of thofe legiflatures, who indifcriminately inflict the punifhment of death for fo
many *different* offences, muft, upon the leaft reflection,
appear confonant to no principle of reafon, and, on
deliberation, will be difcovered to be a direct in-

fcorned to deny his affiftance to the helplefs, and fly to the afylum his independence might have procured him. At once determined to combat an hydra unknown in his former practice,
his fertile genius no fooner furnifhed him with weapons of defence, than his intrepidity to the impending danger infured a
victory, fo far as to have weakened the rapacity of the mon-
fter. From a dear-bought experience, and paid for nearly at
the price of his ufeful life, he had an opportunity to bring forward principles in the healing art—thefe principles he has fince
advanced as juft, from the cleareft theoretical reafoning, and
borne up by the ftrongeft evidences of a fuccefsful practice.
And ftill there are opponents of this philofopher as well as phyfician, who have dared to afcribe to his *vifionary* imagination,
what can only be imputed to a defect in their intellects, or per-
verfion of their hearts. Fortunately, thofe of the latter clafs
enjoy not the potency of Jove, or we might, ere this period,
have feen a Rush proftrately fharing the fate of the *Reftorer* of
Hippolytus.

fringement

fringement on the privileges of mankind. It needs
no demonftration to prove, that the heinous offence
of murdering a fellow-creature muft imprint on the
mind a much ftronger fenfe of refentment, than the
petty offence of ftealing a yard of cloth. The former pictures to the imagination the bafenefs of the
human heart in its deepeft dye, and naturally implants
in the mind an eagernefs to punifh feverely the per-
petrator, while the latter will fimply call forth a fentiment of forrow for the frailties of a brother member,
which might have been checked perhaps in their
operations, had the guardians of his juvenile moments
inftilled into his mind, when tender, the precepts of
moral juftice. Upon what principle, then, can the
fame punifhment for thefe two offences be juftified?
Upon what ground of equity is it fupported? Is
not the general practice of it a direct implication
that there is no diftinction between murder and theft?
And as there does exift a difference, is it not abfurd
in the extreme, nay impolitic, to force upon men a
belief to the contrary? Why then do nations continue bigoted in favour of a practice fo detrimental
to public happinefs, and which long experience has
declared as anfwering the worft of purpofes? Monf-
trous iniquity! Age of contradictions! How much
is it to be lamented, that, in an era of civilization,
fo palpable an inconfiftency fhould exift. The mari-
ner would be deemed a novice, were he to fet an
equal prefs of fail in frefh and in moderate breezes;
the phyfician a quack, to prefcribe the fame remedy
for different difeafes; the lawyer a pretended pro-
feffor, for commencing the fame action for every
injury; and yet the legiflatures of moft countries
(including thofe of feveral of our ftates) who inflict
the penalty of death for murders, burglaries, petty
thefts, &c. without diftinction, are held up as compofed of men felected for their wifdom, humanity,
and juftice. And in what inftances have they difcovered

covered thefe attributes? Their knowledge furely
cannot confift in imitating a fyftem, begotten in tyranny, and fanctioned by error, and cuftom : their
love of the human race is not evidenced by the numerous victims to their laws : and their juftice, I hope,
will not be faid to exift in fuch an ufurpation of
power over the life of an individual.

Independent, then, of the ill policy of capital punifhments, proved by the difadvantages accruing to
communities fince the introduction of them, they
ought not to be permitted in a free government,
inafmuch as it is an encroachment, as juft obferved,
on the rights of individuals. It may feem ftrange,
that the power of a legiflature, appointed by the
nation at large, and who are faid to fpeak the will
of the people, fhould be queftioned, and that laws
paffed by them fhould be deemed unjuft : fuch neverthelefs is the cafe. The idea fo generally accepted,
that a fociety can enact any laws whatever, for
their regulation and benefit, will, upon being viewed
ftrictly, turn out an erroneous one. Although the
fovereignty of a country may exercife all the authority vefted in them, by the common confent of the
governed, yet it fhould be recollected, that they can
hold no more power than their conftituents themfelves could poffefs ; and if they make ufe of any
other, it is affumed. To illuftrate this : Men originally had the privilege of doing whatever they pleafed,
without any kind of reftraint, which was not forbidden by the laws of nature or laws of God, which
we deem their natural liberty. From the numberlefs
inconveniences under which they laboured, by living
without government and laws ; from the expofure of
fome to the depredations of thofe more ftrong and
cunning than others, they were thus early induced to
form themfelves into civil fociety. From a fenfe of
their weakneffes, they were urged to this method of
fecuring to them what they were unable to protect
themfelves ;

themfelves ; and for that purpofe deemed it neceffary
that each member fhould refign a certain proportion
of his natural liberty, in order to enjoy in tranquillity
and fafety the remainder, called his rational or civil
liberty. This portion he threw into the common
ftock, upon an implied condition, that the whole
fhould protect and defend him from one his fuperior
in ftrength, and which they are bound to do, until
he forfeits his protection by refufing to fubmit to the
will of the whole. The amount of all thefe portions
conftituting what we term the fovereign power, and
being vefted in one or many, as the whole fhall think
proper, it hence refults, that nations cannot fucceed
to more privileges than thofe which belonged to the
individuals who compofe them, while in a ftate of
nature. How happens it then, that the fupreme
power of a fociety can fend out of animal exiftence
the tranfgreffor of its decrees ? Life is the moft tranf-
cendent privilege which man can poffibly enjoy. It
is the choiceft gift of his Creator, and beftowed on
him for the exprefs purpofe of anfwering the end of
his creation. That life cannot be taken from him,
unlefs by the exprefs permiffion of more than human
authority, deducible from the laws of nature, or if
you pleafe, my friend, from thofe of revelation. Can
we collect from either of thefe laws, that one man
has dominion over the life of another ?—No—By the
law of nature a man may not even kill his enemy ; he
has only a right over his life in one particular cafe,
and that of an abfolute and extreme neceffity, as
where an attack is made upon him, with an intention
to kill, and his own prefervation depends on the immediate deftruction of his antagonift. But this neceffity cannot exift, if we can otherwife difable a man
from injuring us, by confining his perfon.

Nor can any permiffion revealed to us, authorizing
the punifhment of death, be faid really to exift. Although

though it is juftified by a celebrated writer *, from
the fuppofed precept delivered to Noah, that " whofo
" fheddeth man's blood, by man fhall his blood be
" fhed:" yet I coincide perfectly with Dr. Rufh †,
who in his expofition of this fentence, thinks it to be
" a *prediction* rather than a *law*." We well know,
that the unjuft death or wounding of one perfon, will
be often apt, from different circumftances, fuch as
roufing the indignation or revenge of the relations
and friends of the deceafed, &c. to produce other
bloodfhed : and in a belief that it is not a law, I am
confirmed beyond doubt, when I advert to another
text of fcripture more pofitive, and where we are
exprefsly enjoined an obfervance of the command-
ment, "thou fhalt not kill." Some perhaps may
fupport the juftice of the punifhment of death, under
the law of retaliation, as an eye for an eye, tooth for
a tooth, &c. On this law it is merely neceffary to
obferve, that however expedient Mofes might have
deemed feverity and cruelty for the government of
the Jewifh nation (for they were of all people the
moft profligate in principle, as well as barbarous in
manners, and their leader no lefs diftinguifhed for
his inexorable mandates) ftill the fame policy cannot
be faid to fuit nations, whofe manners have been
meliorated by time, and the influence of the doctrines
of the Prince of Peace. He gave us fo many precepts
of morality and forbearance, that none can affume
the title of his followers, and retain at the fame time
practice and principles which in his divine miffion he
fo directly forbids.—Another thing, we are all taught
to believe, that we have no authority to put a period
to our own exiftence, as being an act contrary to
every principle of morality : if fo, how can we undertake to deprive another of life, unlefs in the fimple

* Judge Blackftone.
† Vide " Inquiry into the Effects of public punifhments upon
criminals and upon fociety."

inftance already mentioned, of felf-defence, the firft law of nature.

As a man then has not a power over his own life in his natural ftate, much lefs over that of another, and as a fociety can hold no other authority, than it derives from the men who compofe it were entitled to in a ftate of nature, it is clear that it cannot put to death any one of its members. But admitting that the power of taking life was vefted in a man while in a ftate of nature, upon what principle is it underftood as transferred to the community he entered into? It has been obferved that the individuals fubfcribed their feveral portions of natural liberty, for the benefit of themfelves. It was a profpect of future convenience, a confideration of comfort and happinefs, which prompted each of them to enter into the compact of fociety. In making a facrifice of what he conceived part of that liberty, it could never be fuppofed that he intended to include his greateft privilege, that of life, a liberty, the foundation of every other bleffing. The portion was refigned in order to fecure the remainder, which neceffarily implies, that *part* only of the thing is difpofed of. But where the whole is conveyed at once, which is his life, how can there exift a remainder? As the original contract then between men to form fociety was only implied, and a profpect of good, a promife of future comfort, the confideration offered by the compact for each of the individual's portion, it follows, that fociety is obligated above all, to preferve the exiftence of its members. So that, take the queftion in whatever view we will, whether we fay, that man in his natural ftate had no privilege of taking the life of another, except for his immediate defence and prefervation; or whether we determine that he had fuch a privilege, we ftill can have no hefitation in declaring, that in the firft cafe the punifhment of death is *tyrannical*, becaufe the power can be derived from nothing human;

and

and in the fecond inftance, that it is *unjuft*, as it cannot be conceived, that man on entering into civil fociety, fhould renounce fo valuable a liberty as life.

The punifhment of death thus afcertained to be an encroachment on the rights of the citizen, I would wifh to go one ftep farther than the legiflature of Pennfylvania—I fhould be happy to obferve it abolifhed even in the cafe of murder : and for this reafon. Murder is the higheft offence which man can poffibly commit ; an action which betrays the depravity of the human heart in its blackeft garb ; a crime directly violating all laws both human and divine, and therefore fhould be punifhed with the fevereft penalty that fociety can inflict. I will not be faid to contradict myfelf, when I affert, that to take life is by no means fufficiently fevere. The principle on which I reprobate the punifhment of death is, that it is impolitic and unjuft ; that it is too fanguinary, and exceeding in proportion the injury proceeding from moft offences, but evidently too mild for the crime of cool and deliberate murder. True is it, that it is the higheft forfeit which can be made, but never can be confidered as the moft painful. What punifhment you will afk. inftead of death can be fubftituted for fo horrid a crime as murder ? The anfwer is obvious : fuch an one as is of longer duration, and calculated to make *repeated* rather than *violent* impreffions ; and which once witneffed, thought of, or defcribed, would always preferve in a perfon's mind a recollection or idea of the fufferer's fituation. This might be effected without infringing the laws of humanity, by a punifhment for life, compounded of equal proportions of hard labour, and folitary confinement, in a dungeon or cell of the defcription I have given you. The murderer is no fooner placed in one of thefe cells, than he finds himfelf in the moft dreary abode the human mind can conceive. Admitted as little as poffible to the fight of his own fpecies ; fojourner amidft, yet a

ftranger

ftranger to all the beauties of variegated nature, his
eyes are gratified by the countenances of none of his
fellow-creatures, excepting of his keeper, and perhaps
a ftranger, whom curiofity might now and then direct
to a view of his lonefome habitation : indulged by no
profpect of the glorious fun vivifying by his benign
influence every part of animated creation, and tinging
in his brightened courfe the etherial manfions ; none
of the illumined planets, purfuing with regularity
through the fpotted firmament, their deftined revolu-
tions. Deaf to all the founds which delight the ear,
the tuneful notes of the feathered fongfters can gain
no admittance into his lonely cell. He hears fcarcely a found, unlefs the majeftic *ordnance of heaven*, or
the daily grating of iron bolts and doors. Thefe,
with the additional confideration of want of every
comfort, render his condition truly miferable. But
even all this might be tolerably fupported, had he not
to encounter an enemy too formidable to fubdue, and
from which there is no retreating. Haraffed by the
weapons of felf-torment ; his foul pierced by the keen
fhafts of confcious guilt ; he attempts, but in vain, to
feek fhelter in thought, for there he finds no afylum.
Daily fwallowing thus the bitter draught of remorfe
and wretchednefs, his wearied frame enjoys but a fhort
refpite, even fhould fleep take poffeffion of his
limbs ; for his mind's reft is at times difturbed by the
fpectres attendant on an unhappy confcience, prefenting themfelves in all the hideous forms, torture of
thought can fuggeft : and when he awakes, 'tis only
to behold in imagination, the angry appearance of
offended majefty. What fituation can be more painful ! What punifhment more proper for a murderer !
Why it is not inflicted by the legiflature of this ftate,
I am at a lofs to account for, unlefs they have im-
bibed that common received opinion, founded on the
Levitical law, that life is the only equivalent for life.
The

The criminal laws of Pennfylvania, have neverthe-lefs approached in the neareft degree to perfection, by abolifhing the punifhment of death for every other crime ; and when we contraft them with thofe of other nations, with what admiration do we behold them. For inftance : the three objects of penal laws, or the ends for which punifhments are defigned, are the *amendment* of the criminal—the *reparation to* the injured fociety or individual—and a *prevention* of the fame offence, by an *example* of the offender. Let us endeavour to difcover, how far the laws of Great Britain, imitated by a great portion of our ftates, accomplifh thefe objects.

Murder, robbery, burglary, forgery, horfe-fteal-ing, and above two hundred other felonies, likewife ftealing a fecond time above the value of twelve pence, are punifhed with death. This puts reforma-tion out of the queftion, as the convict is deprived of life. The reparation to the injured community is none at all, or at any event very trifling, excepting the *body* of a malefactor, in the fingle cafe of mur-der, can be deemed a fatisfaction. The example is not worth mentioning, as affording a fcene of bar-barity and injuftice, often exciting the indignation, but feldom the fear of individuals.

Receiving ftolen goods, perjury, libelling, ufing falfe weights and meafures, or petty thefts under the value of twelve pence, are refpectively punifhed with difgraceful punifhments, fuch as ftanding in the pillory, burning in the hand, and public whipping, which are ftill farther from anfwering any good end. Reftitution by either of thefe methods is equally unattainable, for the government are at every expenfe of fupporting perfons guilty of the offences, while in confinement, trying them, and inflicting the punifhment ; and no fooner do they ftand their time in the pillory, are burnt in the hand, or receive the appointed number of ftripes, than they are once more let loofe upon the community.

community. As for reformation, they are evidently worfe than before : for befides their feelings being hardened, and often utterly deftroyed, from having fuch a ftigma fixed on them (for the reafons given in the former part of this letter) they have at the fame time acquired, while in jail, a habit of indolence (not to mention numerous other vices) which they afterwards find a difficulty in divefting themfelves of. The example is little better than the reft, for what rogue would hefitate to offend, when he knew, that the only rifk run was either of thefe punifhments.

By the laws now of this country, all the ends of punifhment are anfwered. The *reftitution* to injured fociety is produced by the perfonal induftry, labour, and fervices of the convict. The *reformation* is naturally effected, from living a regular, fober, and moral life during his confinement in prifon—from being long initiated into conftant habits of induftry, in following a trade or occupation ; while the certainty of the laws being enforced, by the offender's being brought to juftice, from no interference of an idea of the unjuft meafure of the punifhment, will always operate as a fufficient *example*, and thereby prove a more ample fecurity to the rights of individuals. And even were thefe three grand objects defeated (which on the contrary are daily effected) there is ftill left a pleafant reflection, that without having recourfe to cruelty, the criminal is at any rate prevented from haraffing the community. ·

By the laws of England enforced in other ftates, a variety of tranfgreffions, widely different from each other in their degrees of criminality, fall indifcriminately under one title or crime, and attended with the fame punifhment. Inftance thofe included under the general definition of murder. In this country, it is confined to any kind of wilful, deliberate, and premeditated killing, or to killing occafioned in the perpetration, or attempt to perpetrate, either rape, arfon,

arfon, burglary, or robbery. All other murders are
of the fecond degree.

The meafure of punifhment being fixed by a difcretionary power, vefted in the judges of the court,
is *another* peculiar trait in the juftice of the Pennfylvania code, and which you will readily pronounce fo,
if you advert for a moment to the impracticability of
otherwife proportioning the punifhment to the crime.
For inftance, fuppofe the punifhment for manflaughter, or for murder of the fecond degree, were defined
to be fix years folitary confinement, and twelve years
hard labour. A man may be guilty of one of thefe
crimes, but with a variety of favourable incidents
appearing on the trial, fuch as *the firft or aggravating*
provocation of the deceafed; his death occafioned by a
blow, given upon fudden or violent paffion, &c. Although
a jury, in this cafe, may be well perfuaded, that the
offence is in fome meafure criminal, yet they will
acquit entirely, or recommend to mercy, rather than
expofe a citizen to a punifhment beyond meafure. So,
if a petty theft were to be punifhed with fix months
hard labour, it is evident that it would not be adequate
for an old and troublefome offender. It has long been
a fubject of deep concern to every humane mind, that
in moft countries the meafure of punifhment has in
fome cafes grofsly exceeded, and in others by no
means equalled, the grade of the offender's guilt.—
Too often has a man, convicted of an high degree of
man-killing, for want of a few legal requifites to bring
the crime within the definition of a murder, efcaped
with a verdict of manflaughter, or a trifling finge on
the hand, while one perhaps of fuperior feelings, from
an improper method of fupplying his immediate wants,
renounces his life. Oftner is the convict, from the
kind interpofition of mercy, in extricating him from
the talons of injuftice, induced to believe the *propriety*
of impunity, when, in fact, it was only the conflict
occafioned by the little fway juftice had, which fa-
voured

voured him with an efcape. Whereas here nothing
of the kind can exift. The judge's fentence, according
to the circumftances under which the crime is committed ; in doing which, they take into confideration
the opportunity for vice offered at the time—the
place, age, education, and general good or bad conduct of the delinquent through life—the paffion which
governed him—and in proportion to thefe, and a
variety of other aggravating and extenuating circumftances, fhorten or protract the term of labour or
confinement : fo that no inftance is likely to happen,
of an offender, in the cuftody of the laws efcaping a
merited punifhment. By thefe means juftice will be
impartially adminiftered, and no penalty impofed dif-
proportionate to the offence, unlefs the power fhould
be abufed by the judges. There can be little probability of this taking place, when men, felected for
their judgment, character, and integrity, are generally
called to thofe ftations. And even were it to happen,
the mercy of the executive is always ready to refcue
a citizen from oppreffion. The pardoning power,
however, is feldom or never exerted in any other
inftance, which brings to my recollection a prefage of
Beccaria's, " *Happy the country in which it would be*
" *confidered as dangerous !*" Pennfylvania, then, is
that country. Scarcely a fingle inftance has occurred,
fince the eftablifhment of the new penal fyftem, of a
criminal's fentence being wholly remitted : many
convicts, it is true, receive a mitigation of their punifhment, after being reformed ; yet, till that amendment takes place, they are made to fuffer all the
rigor of their fentences. Nor can any counterfeited
reformation of a prifoner procure the pardon of the
governor. The infpectors, jailer, and keepers, muft
have gradually obferved its progrefs, and even under
the moft favourable circumftances, they never think
of interfering for his releafe, unlefs he has completed
the

the greateſt proportion of his term of labour and confinement.

It would notwithſtanding be more deſirable to annihilate all hopes of remiſſion, after a conviction has once taken place. Executive clemency, in any ſhape, can only be neceſſary in thoſe parts of the world, where laws are unjuſt, and puniſhments cruel and ſevere ; and then, like all other defects in the ſyſtem with which it is engrafted, it ſolemnly publiſhes the uncertainty of the laws, ſilently diſarms them of their ſovereignty, and by extending an act of humanity to a ſingle individual, aſſiſts in throwing down a fabric of public protection, long enervated and tottering with other continued ſhocks of impunity. But in a country where puniſhments are moderate, and meaſured with the guilt of criminals ; whoſe legiſlation beams with juſtice and benevolence, the prerogative of pardons becomes highly pernicious, if exercifed. It is then the duty of a chief magiſtrate to be deaf to every entreaty of mercy, and to learn, that with a rational and mild juriſprudence, the rigorous execution of the laws is the only virtue, which can add to his private dignity a public teſtimony of attachment to the lives and property of his fellow-citizens.

Thus have I endeavoured, my dear Sir, in the foregoing pages, to fulfil the object propoſed. I have, in the firſt place, furniſhed you with as correct an account as lay in my power, of the alteration of the penal laws of Pennſylvania—the cauſes which produced it—and the ſalutary conſequences reſulting from it, in effecting as well the wiſe and humane regulations in the *Philadelphia Priſon*, as the diminution of offences throughout Pennſylvania.

Secondly,

Secondly.—I have been led to confider, among the difadvantages flowing in different ages from fanguinary codes of laws, that they have a tendency to increafe rather than prevent crimes; and brought in fupport of it the experience, firft of the ancient Romans, then of modern European nations, and laftly of our own country.

Thirdly.—I have afcertained, why fevere punifh-ments, thus threatened and held up by a government, are lefs fuccefsful in preventing crimes, than mild and moderate penalties; owing to the certainty of their execution being more precarious, from the humanity of profecutors, the compaffion of juries, judges, &c.

Fourthly.—I have thrown together a few other obfervations on the impolicy of the punifhment of death, from its affording an example, calculated from its barbarity and injuftice, to excite rather the indig-nation than terror of individuals; and from thence flightly touched on the abfurd and inconfiftent conduct of legiflatures, and particularly in their applying the fame remedy or punifhment in all cafes whatfoever.

Fifthly.—I have advanced, that the punifhment of death is tyrannical, inafmuch as no fociety can hold a power over the life of one of its members, when the rights of fociety are derived from thofe of nature, and this right not exifting in a ftate of nature, even over our own lives. And admitting that every man had a power over his own life, that the prefervation of his exiftence, above all others, was the principal induce-ment to his entering into civil fociety.

Sixthly.—I have expreffed a wifh, that the taking of life may even be abolifhed for murder; and pro-pofed a punifhment more proper for the offence.

And

And laftly.—I have, in taking a view of the criminal laws of other countries, further demonftrated
the fuperiority of the Pennfylvanian code; a code,
raifed upon the fundamental principles of reafon and
equity, and which, for the beauty and fymmetry of
its parts, muft ever command the admiration of the
world. How gratifying a circumftance muft it appear
to the tender and humane of every defcription, that
an example is at length given to long deluded mankind, embracing in one view fo many noble objects.
When we obferve too, that it is the Emporium of
Northern America, in which the corner-ftone of fo
grand a fuperftructure has been laid, what pleafure
muft it not afford every friend of freedom !—The
defpotic foil of Italy gave birth to the projector of
the plan, a humane Beccaria : England, it is true,
brought forth a Howard : but it is the clime of Pennfylvania, which can exult in the greateft number of
profelytes to thofe ornaments to philanthropy.—Yes,
it is the public fpirit and perfeverance of Pennfylvania's
fons, which alone feem to call the attention of the
world to the practice of their glorious principles.—
Nor is this the only inftance, in which they have difplayed themfelves in all the excellence of unexampled
virtue. Their exertions have been no lefs indefatigable, in preparing an afylum for the poor and helplefs
of all claffes, and in their foundation and fupport of
charitable inftitutions, unequalled, perhaps, in the
world. Here the forrows of decrepid age are foothed
by the fpeedy relief of a comfortable abode ; the
needy orphan and widow no longer want a parent or
protector ; and no more are heard the diftreffing
ravings of the unhappy maniac, to pierce the ears of
human kind. In fine, it appears, that the genii of
reafon and true philofophy have, after a long and
tedious flight over the regions of the earth, at length
lighted upon this fpot as their refidence ; where, by

F coalefcing

coalefcing with the genius of humanity, they might
be better enabled to lay down principles for the future
regulation of mankind, and extend their influence to
the utmoft bounds of the habitable globe.

With every fentiment of efteem and affection,

Believe me,

My dear Sir,

Your fincere Friend,

R. J. T.

APPENDIX.

APPENDIX.

The following Letter appeared in the City Gazette of CHARLESTON, *on the* 27th *February last, shortly after the foregoing Letter was published.*

Meſſrs. FRENEAU & PAINE,

WITH many of your readers, I participated in the pleaſure naturally excited by the account, publiſhed in your paper, of the wiſe and humane regulations adopted in the Philadelphia priſon, and the abolition of cruel, ſanguinary and diſproportionate puniſhments, in the ſtate of Pennſylvania. Such a ſubject is not unworthy of the *juvenile* pen of its author ; and the ſtyle and manner in which he conveys his ſentiments, evince a happy combination of virtue and talents.

The beneficent effects which flow from a mild penal code, founded in humanity and wiſdom, are perhaps the beſt argument that can be applied to thoſe who are advocates for the neceſſity of rigorous and ſanguinary puniſhments. I conceive it to be a true axiom, that the only object of puniſhment for tranſgreſſions of every deſcription, ought to be the prevention of crime, and the reformation of the

F 2   offender.

offender. For, to fuppofe fociety actuated by a principle of revenge, would be to attribute to it a paffion,
which the moft depraved individual would blufh to
acknowledge himfelf capable of. Yet, to take a view
of penal laws in general, one would be naturally led
to believe, that fanguinary punifhments were the effect
of the moft diabolical revenge, proceeding from the
lawlefs command of an infatiable, fanguinary tyrant.

That the adoption of the penal code of England
in this country, did not proceed from a conviction of
its excellence, it is evident. It was merely the refult
of chance. And it is matter of much regret, that
when this country did form a bafis of government
for itfelf, and began a new era of things, that its
legiflature did not employ itfelf in digefting a criminal
code of laws appropriated to the new principles which
it embraced.

In this code there are upwards of two hundred
offences, wholly diffimilar in guilt, which are deemed
capital, and punifhed with death. Such an inconfiftency is too glaring to pafs unnoticed. And the
frequent executions in England prove the fallacy and
inutility of fanguinary punifhments in preventing
crimes; as the mild regulations of the Quakers of
Pennfylvania prove how much fociety may be bene-
fited by wife and humane laws.

It might, perhaps, be attended with much difficulty
to form a juft fcale of punifhment, which would apply
in all cafes, for every denomination of offences;
perhaps impoffible: but in our penal code there is
infinite room for improvement. And the neceffity of
apportioning, as nearly as poffible, the penalty to the
offence, that is, to the injury that fociety fuftains, is
an object of high importance, and worthy the particular attention of the legiflature of South Carolina.

The effect of a wife fyftem of jurifprudence on the
morals of fociety, is probably not fo well afcertained
as it may be hereafter. Mankind make but flow
advances;

advances ; and the effect of any change is not immediately vifible. But finally the refult of judicious and
humane laws will be to diminifh crimes, and facilitate
the happinefs of the community.

Hiftory, both ancient and modern, tells us that in
all ages, crimes have increafed in proportion to the
feverity of the penalties enacted to prevent them ;
and have decreafed in an equal proportion, by the
amelioration of thofe penalties. This is what experience teaches. But unfortunately for mankind, the
voice of experience has not that influence on their
conduct which it ought to have ; and to this in a confiderable degree they owe their misfortunes.

It is, in a great meafure, owing to a miftaken pre-
dilection in favour of every cuftom which can boaft of
antiquity, that mankind have fo long wandered in the
inexplicable mazes of ignorance, error, and confequent misfortune ; that they prefer favage and barbarous cuftoms, to thofe which experience and wifdom
would recommend. But notwithftanding this deplorable remiffnefs, feemingly incident to human nature,
it is a confolation to the friends of humanity, that
there is an apparent proximity towards improvement
manifefted in every thing. And though the progrefs
of knowledge be flow, it is certain and efficacious, and
cannot readily be fupplanted after it has taken root.

VOLNEY.

Letter from the Author to the Editors of the City Gazette
of CHARLESTON.

Gentlemen,   Philadelphia, *March* 25th, 1796.

THE Gazettes you have thought proper to tranf-
mit me, containing the publication of my *Obfervations on the Philadelphia Prifon, &c.* in a *Letter to a
Friend,* came to hand laft evening ; and permit me,
by this opportunity, to thank you for them, as alfo
for your approbation accompanying them. I confefs
I was not a little furprifed to obferve the letter communicated to the public.

The occafion of thofe obfervations was a vifit to
that inftitution, which gratified me fo much, that I
immediately fat down, and attempted to convey to the
mind of one with whom I have long been in habits of
intimacy and friendfhip, the fame pleafant impreffion
of its wife and humane adminiftration. While fuch
were my intentions, it had not at any one time
occurred to me, that they would have made an appearance in a public print, or I fhould certainly have
not avoided the fending with them fuch proofs, as
might be neceffary to eftablifh the falutary effects
which have iffued from the alteration of the former
penal code of Pennfylvania, and from the new arrangements adopted in confequence of it in the prifon of
this city. This, however, for another opportunity.

The fubject, Gentlemen, is certainly of that nature,
as by no means to have merited the apathy with which
it has heretofore been treated, and efpecially in
American States, whofe governments fhould, of all
others, proceed with the utmoft deliberation towards
the organization of laws, which may affect the life of
a fingle citizen. What then would be more interefting,
than if men of real talents and influence amongft us,
were to devote a fmall degree of attention to the
pleafing tafk—no lefs a one than the preventing the
                                                            ufelefs

ufelefs effufion of human blood ? It is principally from
the aid of thefe characters, that recommendations can
command their juft weight of refpectability. I fhould
be happy to obferve them ftep forward, from the
benefits they might entail on pofterity.

It is, neverthelefs,. a matter of no fmall confolation
to the humane of every defcription, to obferve a work
of reformation gaining ftrength, which *once* matured,
muft from the experience of this country alone, contribute perhaps to the happinefs of millions hereafter.
The General Affembly of New York, have, a few
weeks ago, abolifhed the punifhment of death, for
every crime except murder and treafon. That of
New Jerfey have, on the 18th inftant, fuppreffed it in
moft cafes ; and the legiflatures of other ftates feem fo
far convinced of the importance of the fubject, that
they have directed inquiry to be made, as to the effects
a fimilar meafure would be likely to produce. For
my own part, I have not a doubt but what a con-
geniality of legiflative fentiment, in this refpect, will
foon become general throughout the union ; and
indeed feel a fatisfaction in believing, that the period
is not far diftant, when the unprejudiced of all nations,
will, with one affent, fubfcribe to the juftice and policy
of *mitigation in punifhments.*

With a full perfuafion that the recommendations of
your executive will meet with the approbation of the
legiflature of South Carolina, and a wifh that every
jail government in the world may, like that of the
Philadelphia prifon, reft on the grand truth of,—
" *Vitiorum femina—otium—labore exhauriendum ;*"

Believe, me, Gentlemen, .

With due refpect,

Your obedient fervant,

R. J. T.

Meffrs. Freneau & Paine,
Charlefton, S. Carolina.   *Extract*

*Extract of a Letter on the same subject, dated February
20th, 1796, from a respectable character in London,
holding an appointment under the American Government, to CALEB LOWNES, an Inspector of the Prison,
and one of the earliest friends to the reform.*

HOW comes on the Philadelphia Penitentiary
House? I see the success of your plan highly
spoken of in the Governor's address to the legislature,
which gives me sincere and lively pleasure.—I rejoice
to find also, that the attention of Congress has been
turned to the subject—that there is a prospect of their
penal code being ameliorated, and of the same respect
being paid, in the laws of the Union, to the preservation of life, and the *prevention* of crimes, as in the
laws of individual states.   What a reflection is it on
the humanity, nay, indeed, on the wisdom and policy of the rulers of states and nations, that so little
attention should have been given, and such faint exertions made, to *reform* rather than to *extirpate*—to
reclaim rather than to *punish!* I most ardently hope,
that we may both live to see the day (and that at no
distant period) when, by the diffusion of knowledge
—the increasing influence of the most liberal philanthropy—but more especially by a true *understanding*
and *practice* of genuine unadulterated Christianity,
man may learn to love and *do good* to his fellow-man—
and the *punishment of death* be for ever abolished.

Convinced as I am, that society has *no right* to take
away the life of a citizen, I am also persuaded, that
the period is rapidly approaching, when governments
will think it as *impolitic* as it is wrong, to exercise this
assumed power.

PUNISHMENTS for several Heinous Offences, as established by the Laws of *Pennsylvania*.

CRIMES.	QUALITY of PUNISHMENT.	QUANTUM of PUNISHMENT. For any Period not exceeding 21, nor less than 10 Years.	
Rape - - - - - -	A Compound of Hard Labour and Solitary Confinement.	Ditto 18,	Ditto 5
Murder of the second Degree—Petit Treason - -	Ditto	Ditto 15,	Ditto 4
Counterfeiting, or uttering counterfeit Gold or Silver Coin—Forging or uttering forged Bank Notes	Ditto		
High Treason - -	Ditto	Ditto 12,	Ditto 6
Arson - - - -	Ditto	Ditto 12,	Ditto 5
Maliciously maiming—voluntary Manslaughter - -	Ditto	Ditto 10,	Ditto 2
Burglary—Robbery—Crimes against Nature - - -	Hard Labour,	Ditto 10,	
Horse Stealing - - -	Ditto	Ditto 7,	

N. B. The Solitary Confinement cannot be less than one-twelfth, nor exceed one-half, of the whole Term of Confinement. *Maliciously maiming*, besides Hard labour, and Solitary Confinement, is attended with a Fine, not to exceed 1000 Dollars, three-fourths of which to go to the party grieved.—For *Horse Stealing* likewise, and *all Larcenies*, there must be a Reparation to the Value of the Thing stolen, and also a Fine to the Commonwealth.

A TABLE

A TABLE of OFFENCES committed in the City and County of PHILADELPHIA, from Jan. 1, 1787, to June, 1791, being a Period of the last 4 Years and 5 Months under the old Criminal System.

OFFENCES COMMITTED.

PERIODS.	Murder	Burglary	Robbery	Forgery	Counterfeiting	Horse Stealing	Bigamy	Larceny	Misdemeanors 1st Degree	Misdemeanors 2d Degree	Receiving stolen Goods 1st Degree	Receiving stolen Goods 2d Degree	Defrauding	Violent Assault to kill	Harbouring Convicts	Keeping disorderly Houses	Total Number of Offences
From Jan. 1st, 1787, to May 1st, 1788,		20	20	5				122	2	6	7	2				3	186
May 1st, 1788, to May 1st, 1789,		24	5					57		4	9	3		5	2	1	113
May 1st, 1789, to May 1st, 1790,	6	13	10		3	4		82	2	3	3	1	3	3	3	2	134
May 1st, 1790, to June, 1791.	3	20	5		3	5	1	113			7					4	161
																	594

N. B. Deduct from this Table 12 Offences, which ought more properly be put down to other Counties.

A TABLE

A TABLE of OFFENCES committed in the State of PENNSYLVANIA, from June, 1791, to Oct. 27, 1795, being a Period of the first four Years and five Months under the New System of Laws.

OFFENCES COMMITTED.

PERIODS.	Manslaughter	Rape	Arson	Bigamy	Burglary	Robbery	Forgery	Counterfeiting	Horse Stealing	Larceny	Misdemeanors 1st Degree	Misdemeanors 2d Degree	Receiving stolen Goods 1st Degree	Receiving stolen Goods 2d Degree	Defrauding	Keeping Disorderly Houses	Concealing the Death of a Ballard Child	Total Number of Offences
From June, 1791, to June, 1792	1				2	2	7	1	7	42					2			65
June, 1792, to June, 1793	2				11	1		1	1	40	1		1		1			61
June, 1793, to June, 1794	1		1		2		3		15	34		1		1		2		61
June, 1794, to 27 Oct. 1795	1	1	1	1	1	2	3	3	5	88	2	2		2		2	1	114
																		301

N. B.—Since the commencement of this Period of four Years and five Months, the Convicts from all the different Counties in the State have been sent to the Prison of Philadelphia. Formerly they were not.

Remarks

Remarks on the two foregoing Tables of Crimes.

THESE are tables of crimes and not criminals,
There were 484 perfons convicted of the foregoing offences, under the *law for public and difgraceful
treatment*—and 245 under the *prefent* fyftem (fo far
only it muft be remembered as March, 1795), making
in the whole 729—of thefe 27 only have been again
convicted, 15 men and 12 women—and but 5 of the
729 have been convicted a *fecond* time for the laft
four years under the new fyftem, 1 for horfe-ftealing
and 4 for larcenies ; whereas the books of the prifon
will fhew that 184 perfons were frequently convicted
under the old law ; all of whom had been conftantly
engaged in committing offences againft fociety, and
followed no other mode of living, and had frequently
broke jail or efcaped from their keepers—94 were
convicted divers times for committing 249 crimes,
and chiefly of the moft daring and dangerous nature,
being confeffedly the moft atrocious characters in the
country.   There were others of equally dangerous
characters, who do not appear to have been convicted
more than once, but who were well known to have
been engaged in the bufinefs regularly ; of thefe
there were about 80, the remaining 10 do not appear
to have been quite fo bad.   The jail books again
prove, that of 594 crimes committed in four years
under the old law, 346 were committed by thefe 184
characters ; a number fufficient to difturb any community ; and it appears that they were the principal
agents in the bufinefs—67 broke jail, and 37 efcaped
from their keepers, and when at work abroad.
Averaging the 94 who were re-convicted twice and
oftener, at three times, will make 282 out of 484, and
fay 90 others, who are known to have been engaged
in this work, will give the greater part of the offenders
who had fo long troubled fociety.

                                                  From

From thefe tables alone it appears, that fince the late improvements in the penal code, offences have diminifhed in a proportion of about one half, and when we recollect, that the firft table contains the offences of the city and county of Philadelphia only, we may pronounce that they have decreafed throughout the whole ftate nearly two-thirds—The two periods are equal, and the latter commences from 1791, from the new difcipline not having taken place previous to that time. The moft material point gained with refpect to offences, is the diminution of the moft heinous ones, which are ftill in a greater proportion. They ftand in the tables as follows :

	Under the old Syftem in the City and County.	Under the new Syftem in the whole State.
Burglary . . .	77	16*
Robbery . . .	39	5.
Murder . . .	9	0
Arfon	0	1
Rape	0	1
Bigamy . . .	1	1
Total	126	24

The following Facts early furnifhed by Mr. Lownes, were omitted by the Author when the Sheets in which they might have been more properly introduced had gone to Prefs. Thinking them interefting, he has preferred placing them out of Order, to withholding them from the Public.

AT the time of the yellow fever, in 1793, great difficulty was found in obtaining nurfes and attendants for the fick at Bufh-hill hofpital. Recourfe

* Only 4 of thefe 16, were committed in the City and County.

was had to the prifon. The requeft was made, and
the apparent danger ftated to the convicts. As many
offered as were wanted—They continued faithful till
the dreadful fcene was clofed—none of them making
a demand for their fervices till all were difcharged.

One man committed for a burglary, who had feven
years to ferve, obferved, when the requeft was made
to him, that having offended fociety, he would be
happy to render it fome fervices for the injury; and
if they could only place a confidence in him, he
would go with cheerfulnefs.—He went—he never
left it but once, and then by permiffion to obtain
fome articles in the city. His conduct was fo remarkable as to engage the attention of the managers,
who made him a deputy-fteward; gave him the
charge of the doors, to prevent improper perfons
from going into the hofpital, to preferve order in and
about the houfe, and to fee that nothing came to or
went from it improperly. He was paid, and after
receiving an extra compenfation, at his difcharge
married one of the nurfes. Another man, convicted
of a robbery, was taken out for the purpofe of attending a horfe and cart, to bring fuch provifions
from the vicinity of the city, as were there depofited
for the ufe of the poor, by thofe who were afraid to
come in. He had the fole charge of the cart and
conveying the articles, for the whole period. He
had many years to ferve, and might at any time have
departed with the horfe, cart, and provifions. He
defpifed, however, fuch a breach of truft, and returned to the prifon. He was foon after pardoned,
with the thanks of the infpectors.

Another inftance of the good conduct of the prifoners during the ficknefs, happened among the women. When requeft was made of them to give up
their bedfteads, for the ufe of the fick at the hofpital,
they *cheerfully offered* even their bedding, &c. When
a fimilar requeft was made to the debtors, they *all
refufed.*

A criminal,

A criminal, one of the defperate gangs who had fo long infefted the vicinity of Philadelphia, for feveral years before the alteration of the fyftem, on being difcharged, called upon one of the infpectors, and addreffed him in the following manner : " Mr. ——, I " have called to return you my thanks, for your kind- " nefs to me while under fentence, and to perform a " duty which I think I owe to fociety, it being all in my " power at this time to afford. You know my con- " duct and my character have been once bad and loft, " and therefore whatever I might fay would have " but little weight was I not now at liberty. Purfue " your prefent plan, you will have neither burglaries " nor robberies in this place." He then ftated the fentiments held by thofe characters who had devoted themfelves to this mode of life, and the plans generally purfued by them. The certainty of conviction and the execution of the fentence—the *privations*, temperance, order, labour, &c. was more to be dreaded than any thing they had ever experienced.— He obferved at parting, that he fhould never trouble the infpectors more. This promife has been fully complied with.

ABSTRACTS